CW00431413

CHRISTIAN TRAINING F

EXPLORING THE NEW TESTAMENT

a traveller's guide to Acts–Revelation

George Wieland

Published by
The Baptist Union of Great Britain
April 1992

Except where acknowledged, all photographs are reproductions of full colour slides from sets produced by Mr Maurice Thompson of **Bible Scene Slide Tours.** The publishers acknowledge with gratitude permission to reproduce these photographs.

Further details of the services offered by Bible Scene Slide Tours may be had from: 26 Home Close, Sharnbrook, Bedford MK44 1PQ. Telephone No: 0234 781946.

Christian Training Programme Manual

B3

Designed, typeset and produced for the Baptist Union of Great Britain by
Gem Publishing Company, Brightwell, Wallingford, Oxfordshire.

Printed in Great Britain by Swindon Press Limited, Swindon, Wiltshire.

CONTENTS

EDITOR'S PREFACE

Most people enjoy a good adventure, and why not! This study guide is for those willing to embark on the adventure of exploring the New Testament. It is designed chiefly for first-time travellers, for whom the territory is unfamiliar and possibly bewildering. But seasoned explorers of the New Testament will also find great profit from this travel guide.

The material may be used in a variety of ways.

CTP COURSE

You may have chosen this manual as part of your studies in the Christian Training Programme Diploma, Lay Preacher's Certificate or Lay Pastor's Certificate courses. If so, you will need to work your way through the units with the guidance and encouragement of your tutor and adviser. The assignments you will need to complete are found on the leaflet enclosed with the manual when you enrolled. There are other suggestions for reflection and thought in the manual which you will find of interest, but you will be assessed only on your response to the assignments.

GROUP STUDY

You may have opportunity to use the material in a group and we commend this practice. The book contains many suggestsion for group discussion and for drawing out the practical application of the New Testament books. It is a proven fact that adults learn best in the mutual sharing of groups; so if it is possible to work through this material with others, you will be well rewarded.

PERSONAL INTEREST AND STUDY

There will be others who are neither working on a CTP course nor part of a group, but who will find this manual helpful in personal Bible study. No one who embarks on the journey to which this book calls will be disappointed, and this study guide will prove a valuable reference book along the way.

'TO THINK ABOUT' SECTIONS

In the first half of this study guide there are several TO THINK ABOUT sections which suggest both ways of reading a New Testament book and the questions you might ask as you come to study it. In the latter half of the study guide these sections are deliberately less frequent. You are left to follow the same pattern and ask similar questions as in the earlier units. The Exploring Further sections also point you in the direction of particular issues you may be interested to think through.

However you use this manual, our hope is that you will find the journey worthwhile, the adventure rewarding and this study guide a helpful companion on the journey.

Paul Mortimore
Editor

AUTHOR'S PREFACE

This is not so much a book *about* the New Testament as a companion for the person who wishes to explore these writings for him- or herself. It is **a traveller's guide**, providing information, encouraging the development of necessary skills and suggesting routes and methods of travel, but it is the traveller who must make the journey.

You will not, therefore, find here a comprehensive account of someone else's travels. This book is neither an exhaustive introduction to the New Testament writings nor a commentary. Such works are of great value, and an appendix indicates how they might be used. This guide book, however, sets out to assist the reader of the New Testament in three ways. There is an introduction (**Background Briefing**) to each of the writings, giving such information and comments as will make the journey through the text more fruitful; there are sign-posts for **A Journey through** each New Testament document; and there are suggestions for **Exploring Further** particular themes and issues.

This three-fold pattern will be found throughout, but there is some flexibility in the way it is employed. The first unit, for example, really serves as part of the introduction to all that follows, and the first half of Unit 3, on Paul, provides information which casts light on all the letters explored in Units 3–7. The guidelines for reading through the New Testament material vary according to the nature of each book. For example, the reader is encouraged to think his or her way through Romans fairly meticulously in order to follow the closely reasoned argument, but in Revelation is asked to step back and watch the big picture unfold.

It cannot be stressed too strongly that the crucial activity in working through this guide book is *reading the New Testament itself*. Reading through each letter or other document dealt with does not merely supplement the information given in the introduction, nor is it just a prelude to a detailed examination of specific questions. **To learn to read these documents, really listening to them and understanding them on their own terms, is the aim of this course.** This demands the development of certain skills, and it is these that the study guide seeks to cultivate as it accompanies the reader through the text. Do have patience, therefore, with the step-by-step approach adopted in reading through some of the early letters. As you work through the units you will find that more is taken for granted.

The preparation of this study guide has been, for the author, an exhilerating journey into the world of the first Christians and an enriching and challenging encounter with these primary writings of their faith and ours. The prayer which has accompanied its production is that those who use it may hear the New Testament speaking with greater clarity and relevance, and may be better equipped to open up its message to others.

Various versions of the Bible are referred to throughout this book and the main abbreviations used are as follows:

Authorised Version – AV
Revised Standard Version – RSV
New International Version – NIV
Good News Bible – GNB
Living Bible – LB

George Wieland

Introduction

WHY READ THE NEW TESTAMENT?

Why do you want to read the New Testament? Because you love great literature? Some parts of the New Testament are certainly magnificent in expression and style, but most of it was written in the straightforward everyday Greek current at the time. Perhaps you are interested in Ancient History? The New Testament does provide many fascinating glimpses of the Mediterranean world of the first century AD, but much that an historian would consider important simply does not appear.

Most probably you are among the vast majority of people who turn to the New Testament, not primarily to appreciate it as literature nor to study it as historical source material, but hoping that it has something to say to them today.

THEN AND NOW

Just consider how staggering that expectation is! Take a mixed bag of documents gathered from amongst hundreds produced around the Mediterranean in the second half of the first century AD – four accounts of the saying and doings of a Jewish religious teacher; letters from half a dozen writers, some personal, others addressed to churches or groups of churches; a book of church history; and a collection of visions. Then ponder the fact that 1900 years after they were written these writings are still in print, in fact as the world's current and all-time best-seller. Ponder also that in just about every country in the world people are reading these same twenty-seven documents, now translated into nearly two thousand languages, regarding them as relevant to their diverse societies and of vital importance for their own lives.

Clearly more than literary quality or historical interest is required to explain such a phenomenon. The New Testament is read because in it we hope to hear God's word, eternally relevant, speaking to every age and situation. Many letters, tracts and books were produced in the first century of the Church's life, but there is evidence that from the earliest days there was a discrimination between writings which were of local or temporary value only and those which could be read in worship alongside the Old Testament scriptures. A great council of the Church, meeting at Carthage in AD 397, finally listed the writings which make up the New Testament as we have it today and affirmed that only these and the books of the Old Testament could be 'read in church under the name of divine scripture', but there had already been widespread agreement on the bulk of the canon for over two hundred years.

> **TO THINK ABOUT . . .**
> How would you sum up your reasons for wanting to read and study the New Testament?

PARTICULAR AND TIMELESS

We are dealing, therefore, with writings which transcend the immediate and local circumstances in which they came into being. But for all that they are still real letters addressing concrete situations in a particular place and time. The task of understanding the New Testament and interpreting it for our own day demands that we take seriously both these dimensions. We seek earnestly and honestly to hear God's voice to us in these writings, but we recognise that God used human authors and particular historical occasions to produce them, and that what God has to say to us today through them will not contradict what he said to the original readers. It is sometimes claimed that you can make the Bible mean whatever you like. The dual nature of the New Testament, however, gives us a control by which we can evaluate the innumerable interpretations which undoubtedly there are. No interpretation can be valid which does violence to the original purpose for which the document was brought into being.

> ## TO THINK ABOUT . . .
>
> Recall examples – perhaps the old promise boxes or some sermons – where a New Testament letter was handled without reference 'to the original purpose for which the document was brought into being'.
>
> Did it matter to you then that this was happening? How might the point which is made in these paragraphs affect in the future your understanding of the New Testament and its message?

Discovering what these writings meant to their first-century recipients is therefore the first task.

From there we can begin to translate that meaning into our own very different circumstances. We shall want to know all we can about the world in which the New Testament was written, the structures and ideas with which both writers and readers would have been familiar. We shall be particularly interested in the circumstances which provoked, for example, the writing of letters from an apostle to particular churches. We shall also have to take seriously the nature of the literature itself. Letters, historical narrative and visions in coded symbolic language are very different sorts of writing and require different approaches if each is to be properly understood on its own terms. Again, our aim is to discover the meaning that the writer originally intended.

The first unit is therefore given over to an exploration of the world in which the New Testament was written. We shall then be able to turn to the documents themselves.

CHOOSING A TRANSLATION

The question of which translation of the Bible to use is important. There are a bewildering number available, differing in language and style, and some passages even seem to mean different things in the various versions. And yet all translations set out with the goal of enabling English speakers to understand a book written originally in Hebrew, Aramaic or Greek.

> ## TO THINK ABOUT . . .
>
> With which translation of the Bible do you feel most comfortable? What factors have contributed to shaping your preference?
>
> E.g. – a knowledge of the Greek.
>   – the version used in your church.
>   – a liking for the language and style.
>   – easier to understand than other versions.
>   – some other factor(s).

This is a complex task. The meaning of a sentence in a foreign language cannot be discovered

simply by looking up the words in a dictionary. Words mean different things in different contexts, and meaning is communicated not only by the choice of the particular words but by how they are placed in the sentence. Different languages organise their sentences in different ways and have their own ways of conveying emphasis and other effects. For this reason the translation which keeps closely to the word order of the original language, attempting to provide precise English equivalents for each Greek word, may in fact obscure the point for English readers who are not familiar with the conventions of Greek grammar!

On the other hand, a translator may use the natural structures of the English language to express what the biblical writer intended to say. He may do this with the intention that the same impact is made on modern readers as was made on those to whom it was first addressed. But in this case the translator has to decide what exactly the point was, a judgement that often has as much to do with theology as linguistics. With the 'word-for-word' approach at least the reader can see for him- or herself where more than one interpretation is possible, but with the 'idea-for-idea' approach the reader is limited to the interpretation of the translator.

Then the translator must consider the culture in and for which the original writings were produced and how to bridge the considerable gap between that and today's culture. Does he reproduce accurately such items as weights and measures, units of currency, greetings and other forms of expression which the original readers would have understood but are unfamiliar to modern readers, or does he look for modern equivalents? If he chooses the first option, the reader has to acquire some background knowledge in order to understand the point being made, but when that knowledge is acquired the point comes across with its original force. If the second approach is taken, the translation makes sense immediately to the reader, but it may have lost some nuance of meaning which the original conveyed.

ROMANS 8:15 – AN EXAMPLE

Let us take one example which demonstrates the differing approaches at work. Compare the versions of **Romans 8:15** set out below.

How can there be such different versions of the same Greek sentence?! We shall look at two points on which they differ: the terms 'the spirit' and 'Abba'.

The Spirit

The **AV** translates word for word, keeping almost exactly to the order of words in the Greek sentence. That leaves us, however, with the difficult phrases, 'spirit of bondage again to fear' and 'Spirit of adoption'. Whatever they may mean, that is not how an English writer would express it!

The 'free' translations, like **GNB** and **LB**, attempt to communicate the idea in understandable English, but in this case they have reached different conclusions as to what the idea is! **GNB** has recognised that in New Testament Greek phrases like 'spirit of bondage [or slavery]' can be used to express something produced by the spirit. So more natural English expressions would be 'spirit that makes you slaves' and 'Spirit that makes you sons'. This would give a translation like, 'You have not received a spirit that makes you slaves . . . but a Spirit that makes you sons . . .' The translator has decided, however, that this is still not clear enough to convey Paul's meaning. He has made a judgement that Paul is speaking about the Holy Spirit and what he does for and in Christians, contrasting what the Spirit does not do with what he actually does, and so he tries to get this across in his translation. So that the point cannot be missed, he has felt free to alter not only the word order but even the words, putting 'God has given' in place of Paul's 'you have received'.

LB, on the other hand, has opted for another interpretation of the 'spirit of . . .' phrases. They could refer to inner attitudes. This translator tries to communicate the contrast between the inner attitude of the slave and the inner

For ye have not received the spirit of bondage again to fear; but ye have received the Spirit of adoption, whereby we cry, Abba, Father.	For you did not receive a spirit that makes you a slave again to fear, but you received the Spirit of sonship. And by him we cry, 'Abba, Father'.	For the Spirit that God has given you does not make you slaves and cause you to be afraid; instead, the Spirit makes you God's children, and by the Spirit's power we cry out to God, 'Father! my Father!'	And so we should not be like cringing, fearful slaves, but we should behave like God's very own children, adopted into the bosom of his family, and calling to him, 'Father, Father'.
Authorised Version	**New International Version**	**Good News Bible**	**Living Bible**

attitude of the child of God, and the word 'spirit' does not appear at all in his version. He has also judged that although the sentence in Greek simply states as a fact what the Christians had received, Paul's intention was to urge them to adopt the attitude of children of God. He therefore expresses it not as a statement but as an exhortation, 'we should . . .'.

NIV, like **AV**, follows the Greek fairly closely. It finds an equivalent expression for 'a spirit of slavery', rendering it 'a spirit that makes you a slave'. But it keeps the Greek form for the second phrase, 'the Spirit of sonship', since although that is not a natural English form and may leave the reader wondering exactly what it means, any other rendering, such as 'the Spirit who makes you sons', would limit the meaning too much.

Abba

The translations also differ on the treatment of the term 'Abba'. Even in the original Greek this was a foreign word, being the intimate term by which a Jewish child in Aramaic-speaking Palestine would address his or her father. Although he was writing in Greek, Paul gave the Aramaic term 'Abba' and then by way of explanation, for the benefit of any readers who would not understand it, he followed it with 'Pater', the Greek word for 'Father'. He evidently saw a dimension of meaning in the Aramaic term which was not fully communicated in the Greek word, so he considered it worth using, even if it required an explanation. For that reason **AV** and **NIV** also use it, but **GNB** and **LB**, setting out to remove any obstacle to a clear understanding of the Bible, simply translate 'Abba' as 'Father' (though **GNB** tries to give something of the flavour of the original with the phrase, 'Father! my Father!').

EVALUATION

The various approaches have their own strengths and weaknesses. The 'free' translations are easy to read, and express ideas clearly and often vividly in terms which the modern English-speaking world can readily understand. The disadvantage is that they often represent just one of a number of possible interpretations of the original language, and sometimes only part of the idea. Such translations are usually the work of one person, and therefore inevitably it is his particular understanding of the Bible which comes across.

The more 'literal' translations demand more of the reader, and therefore some of the immediate impact may be lost, but they preserve more of the possibilities inherent in the original writings.

For our purposes in this course, one of the latter such as **NIV** or **RSV** should be the main resource, but various 'free' translations can be used very profitably alongside it, especially when reading a letter through at one sitting to get an overview of its contents. They can also sometimes provide helpful insights into the meaning of particular passages.

THE GREEK TEXTS

We have not touched on another crucial issue, that of the Greek text used by the translators, because the task of comparing the hundreds of ancient manuscripts available and deciding which are the most reliable is extremely technical and well beyond the scope of this course. We just have to listen to the experts! It is helpful, however, to be aware that some of the differences between translations are due to differences of opinion as to what is the original text. We can also note that in the 400 years since the Authorised Version was produced many important manuscripts have come to light. These take us much closer to the original documents than the products of centuries of copying which the Authorised Version translators had available to them.

Therefore, quite apart from the differences between Jacobean English and modern English, which make the Authorised Version difficult to understand, it is wiser to use one of the modern versions which are based on more accurate texts.

UNIT 1

The World of the New Testament

ITS GEOGRAPHICAL EXTENT

The list of those present in Jerusalem on the Day of Pentecost (Acts 2:9–11) gives some indication of the geographical spread of the New Testament world. As these visitors returned to their homes, the news would have been carried into North Africa, Egypt and Arabia, up into Asia Minor and across to Europe. This was the Mediterranean world in which, because of her geographical position, Palestine played a central role.

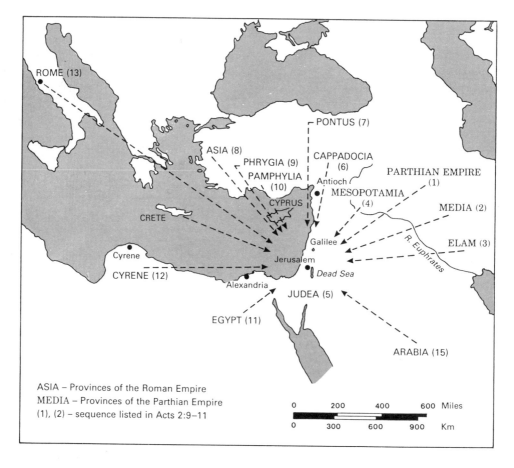

The map shows the locations listed in Acts 2:9–11 from which came the people who were present in Jerusalem on the Day of Pentecost.

The Parthian Empire lay to the east of the river Euphrates.

THE ROMAN EMPIRE

THE EMPIRE'S RISE

In political terms the territory described above roughly marked the boundaries of the Roman Empire. The Old Testament closes with the book of Malachi, who spoke to the Jewish community which had returned from exile under the protection of the Persian Empire. A century later the young Greek ruler Alexander the Great overthrew the Persian occupiers of his native Macedonia and began a campaign of military conquest which took him throughout the known world. Palestine came under his control in 330 BC. Alexander did not live long to enjoy his success, and his vast empire was divided up amongst four of his generals.

Alexander the Great, whose immense influence continued on into the first-century world, not least through the Greek language which he encouraged as the common language throughout the lands he conquered.

Palestine again fell between rival power blocs. For over a century the land was ruled from Egypt in the South-West, but in 198 BC the ruler of Syria, in the East, won control of Palestine. The Syrian rulers showed little sympathy for the Jewish religion, and the repressive measures taken by King Antiochus IV 'Epiphanes' provoked the violent and bitter rebellion known as the Maccabean Revolt: the family of Judas Maccabaeus were in the forefront of the movement.

A century of religious and political independence for the Jewish state ensued, during which the northern territories of Samaria and Galilee were brought within its jurisdiction. In this period, however, Rome's military power was spreading through the Mediterranean world, and in 63 BC a Jewish ruler asked the Roman general Pompey to intervene in a dispute with a rival. Pompey did not stop at that. From the time that his armies entered Jerusalem, Palestine was effectively subject to Rome.

LIFE IN THE EMPIRE

Events recorded in the New Testament, therefore, took place in a world dominated politically by the Roman Empire. Although local life and customs continued, the great fact of Empire was inescapable.

○ **Roman colonies** were established, and the privileges of Roman citizenship were highly prized.
○ **Roman garrisons** were a feature of most major towns, enforcing Rome's rule but also policing the areas and providing some security.
○ **Travel became easier** as new roads were built and the Mediterranean Sea was cleared of pirates.
○ **An effective postal system** improved communications and encouraged the development of letter-writing; new ideas and fads spread quickly.
○ Everyone complained of the **high taxation**, a burden made worse by the profits reaped by the local tax collectors.
○ Economically, the empire was built on the labour provided by **the slave system**. Prob-

ably less than half the population was free, and the households of free citizens were swollen with slaves from peoples conquered by the Roman armies or forced into slavery by poverty. In addition to the menial tasks which we tend to associate with slavery, Roman slaves served as teachers, philosophers, accountants, household managers, doctors and in all manner of skilled occupations.

The '**Pax Romana**' brought undoubted political stability, but this was a vast, changing, frightening world, and many of its inhabitants felt a deep inner turbulence and insecurity.

ADMINISTRATION OF THE EMPIRE

Methods of administering the Empire varied according to local circumstances. In his Gospel and Acts Luke provides rare glimpses of different types of Roman provincial government. In Palestine Herod 'The Great', son of a half-Jewish politician, Antipater, was given the title of King. He consolidated his control of Palestine by a combination of diplomatic manoevering – he built both the magnificant temple in Jerusalem and a temple to the Roman Emperor Augustus at Samaria – and strenuous suppression of any opposition, real or imaginary.

This was the Herod who ruthlessly ordered the murder of all baby boys in Bethlehem, terrified of any rival 'king of the Jews' (Matthew 2:16). He himself died shortly afterwards and for the next half-century parts of Herod's kingdom were governed by his descendants. Other areas came under the control of Roman 'procurators' (middle-ranking governors) such as Pontius Pilate.

The central authority, however, lay in Rome, in the person of the Emperor, and the events and writing of the New Testament took place during the reigns of eleven such emperors. We could set this out in chart form as opposite.

The Appian Way, an example of the network of roads which made possible rapid communication throughout the Empire and by which the Romans exercised their influence. The Apostle Paul completed his journey to Rome along this highway (Acts 28:15).

Dates	Emperor	New Testament references	Events	New Testament Writings*
30 BC–AD 14	Augustus	Luke 2:1	Birth of Christ	
AD 14–37	Tiberius	Luke 3:1	Ministry of John the Baptist Ministry, death and resurrection of Jesus Pentecost Conversion of Paul	
AD 37–41	Caligula			
AD 41–54	Claudius	Acts 11:28; 18:2	Severe famine Jews expelled from Rome Paul's missionary work Church Council at Jerusalem (Acts 15)	Galatians; 1 Thessalonians; 2 Thessalonians
AD 54–68	Nero	Acts 25:10–12; 27:24 ('Caesar')	Paul's final mission, imprisonment & trial, and execution (?) Fire in Rome followed by persecution	1 Corinthians; 2 Corinthians; Romans; Ephesians; Colossians; Philemon; Philippians; 1 Timothy; Titus; 2 Timothy; 1 Peter; James; Hebrews
AD 68	Galba			
AD 69	Otho			
AD 69	Vitellius			
AD 69–79	Vespasian		Siege and destruction of Jerusalem (AD 70)	Jude; Acts
AD 79–81	Titus			
AD 81–96	Domitian		Persecution John exiled to Patmos (AD 90–95)	1, 2, 3 John; Revelation
AD 96–98	Nerva			
AD 98–117	Trajan		Death of John (?)	

* *These dates are in many cases uncertain.*

GREEK CIVILIZATION

The New Testament world was dominated politically by the Roman Empire. It was, however, not Roman but Greek culture which bonded the many peoples and states within it into one entity.

COMMON LANGUAGE AND INSTITUTIONS

Alexander the Great had well understood the importance of a common language, and had encouraged the teaching of Greek in the lands which he conquered. By New Testament times the spread of *koine* ('common') Greek was so complete that it was even the everyday language of the city of Rome. Local languages survived – in Palestine, Aramaic, a language related to Hebrew, was spoken – but practically everywhere in the Roman Empire, Greek was understood.

Not only the Greek language but also many of the ideas and institutions which had developed in the period of Greek supremacy were adopted by the Roman conquerors. The New Testament provides evidence of Greek structures of government in the cities of Asia Minor, scene of the great missionary expansion of the Church.

'VERY RELIGIOUS' CULTURE

It is also clear from the book of Acts and the New Testament letters that the first-century world was, in Paul's words, 'very religious' (Acts 17:22). Perhaps this is hardly surprising. We have already noted that it could be very unsettling to live in this world. As frontiers swept back and people became more aware than ever before of the vastness of this empire of which they were part, many felt lost, powerless and frightened, needing something which could give them a sense of identity and belonging. There was a hunger for supernatural power that could be experienced and used, and a thirst for some hidden knowledge that would make sense of their lives.

The old gods of Greece and Rome still had their adherents, but many were dissatisfied with them. The rites were formal, and many sought a religion more emotionally satisfying; the legends of the gods and their activities met with the disapproval of philosophers concerned for higher ethical standards. Everywhere there were local gods and goddesses. In many places they were simply linked with the name of some Greek or Roman god and continued to be worshipped as before, but in the eyes of some they lost credibility when the people supposedly under their protection were overrun by the advancing imperial armies.

These studies of children are Greek work. They are votive statues taken from the sanctuary of Eliethyia, goddess of childbirth.

There was therefore a widespread willingness to explore new forms of religious experience. From the East came religions with an aura of mystery and emotional intensity. Astrology, magic, demon-worship and other forms of occult practice fascinated many. There was a growth in the popularity of so-called 'mystery religions', offering personal salvation through secret knowledge, gained by rites of initiation which often portrayed the death and rebirth of a god.

GNOSTICISM

From various religious and philosophical sources, ideas were developed which later came together in a new religious movement which we know as Gnosticism. According to these ideas there were two distinct worlds: the world of matter, which was evil, and the world of spirit, which was good. Man, though tied to the world of matter through his physical body, had within himself a 'divine spark', his soul, which sought release by acquiring secret knowledge through mystical experience.

According to this view it was unthinkable that the highest god could have anything to do with the evil world of matter: there had to be many levels of spiritual being, each a little less divine than the previous one, until you eventually found one so corrupt that it could be in contact with the world. The actual creator of the world could not, then, have been the highest God: he must have been a lesser being who, according to some teachers, was himself evil.

For further discussion of Gnosticism see pages 102–3.

EMPEROR WORSHIP

In addition to all this, the first century saw the growth of emperor worship. It had long been an Eastern practice to honour rulers with such titles as 'Lord', 'Saviour' or 'God Manifest', and in the East such worship was now accorded to the new Roman rulers. Elsewhere in the Empire little was made of this at first, but emperors increasingly sought and exploited divine status. Finally, the emperor Domitian (AD 81–96) demanded such worship as a duty of all citizens, thus presenting Christians with a clear choice of allegiance: who was Lord, Caesar or Jesus Christ?

GREEK PHILOSOPHY

The spread of Greek language and the improvement in communications carried Greek philosophy throughout the ancient world. The 'Golden Age' of classical Greece in the fourth and third centuries BC had produced thinkers such as Plato, Socrates and Aristotle. Their ideas had been studied and developed, and throughout the first-century world philosphers and teachers set up their schools and tried to make sense of life and show people how to live – for philosphy was often more practical than abstract, concerned with morals and values.

JUDAISM

Jesus was a Jew, as were the apostles. Jesus' ministry, except for the occasional foray into neighbouring provinces, took place in Palestine; he died, was buried and rose again in Jerusalem, and there the Church was born. Jesus claimed that he was the fulfilment of God's promises to the Jewish people, and that the Jewish scriptures spoke of him. Almost all the writers of the New Testament were Jews. Some knowledge of Judaism will therefore help us to understand the New Testament.

The first point to note is that 'the Jews' in New Testament times were not all alike. Because the Gospels are set in Palestine and the Pharisees were prominent in encounters with Jesus, we could get the impression that all Jews lived in Palestine and that the Pharisees were typical of the Jews as a whole.

THE DIASPORA

Wrong on both counts! In fact in the first century nearly three quarters of all Jews lived outside Palestine. They were known as the Jews of the Diaspora ('Dispersion'), spread throughout the ancient world from the days of the Babylonian Exile onwards. Most major cities had a Jewish community and in some, such as Alexandria in Egypt, they had prospered and received privileges.

By the first century AD few of these Jews could speak Hebrew. They used a Greek translation of the Old Testament, the *Septuagint*, which also made the Jewish faith more accessible to their Gentile neighbours, many of whom found the worship of one God and the high moral standards of Judaism very attractive, in contrast with the confusing multiplicity of gods and the general decadence which they saw elsewhere. Consequently many became proselytes (the term for Gentiles who adopted Judaism), and others who did not want to go as far as that worshipped God and accepted Jewish moral teaching; they were known as God-fearers.

JERUSALEM AND THE TEMPLE

Despite the Diaspora, Jerusalem, and in particular the Temple, continued to be at the heart of Jewish religious life. Here the daily worship went on with morning and evening sacrifices, and the ritual offerings and purifications which marked many of life's events for a religious Jew were made. When Jesus was born a magnificent new temple, begun by King Herod the Great fifteen years earlier, was in use, though still under construction.

Jerusalem was always crowded during the great festivals, especially the Passover, Pentecost and the Day of Atonement. Then the Temple would be thronged with people. There would be an awesome stillness in the innermost shrine, a magnificent building fifty metres high of cream-coloured stone decorated with gold and housing the Holy Place, where the priests offered incense. Still further in was the Holy of Holies, which the High Priest entered only once a year, on the Day of Atonement.

Outside, however, there would be a hubbub of noise and activity. In front of the sanctuary porch was the great altar where the priests offered sacrifices, watched by the men. Beyond that was the Court of the Women, and outside the inner walled area was the Court of the Gentiles which had in practice been taken over by money-changers and traders supplying official currency and approved livestock for temple taxes and offerings. Under the shade of the colonnades around the walls several groups of people clustered around various religious teachers.

The site of Herod's Temple in Jerusalem, dominated now by the mosque known as The Dome of the Rock.

THE SYNAGOGUE

Of course, not all Jews had access to the Temple. This problem had been faced in the time of the Exile, when the Jews had to find ways of preserving and practising their faith in alien lands. This was achieved largely by the development of the Synagogue. The exiled Jews needed some focus for worship, instruction in the Law and the education of their children, and the organisation of their life as a Jewish community.

The synagogues, or 'gatherings', fulfilled these functions. Meeting houses were built and a standard pattern of synagogue life developed. As sacrifices could only be offered in the Temple there was no such ritual in synagogue worship, but regular Sabbath worship developed incorporating the reading of Scripture, a sermon and prayers. Each synagogue had a ruler and elders whose role extended beyond the conduct of the services to administration of community affairs. They had power to enforce their judgements with corporal punishment and excommunication.

So successful was the synagogue system that even those Jews who returned to Judea after the Exile continued to build their lives around it. In New Testament times there were around 400 synagogues in Jerusalem alone, and they were found in every major city – and not a few minor ones – in the Roman Empire. They proved to be a natural launch-pad for evangelism when the Church set out to take the gospel throughout the world.

JUDAISM AND GREEK CULTURE

Naturally enough the settling of Jews as far apart as North Africa and Europe produced considerable diversity in how they lived out their faith. In particular, there was a divergence of attitude regarding how far Judaism should accommodate itself to the prevalent Greek culture. Many were happy to worship in Greek and some tried to find common ground between the Old Testament scriptures and Greek philosophy; others resisted Greek influence and struggled in an alien environment to conserve what they regarded as the purity of their own faith and culture.

MAJOR GROUPS IN JUDAISM

Uniformity was no more evident among the Jews who lived in Palestine. All Jews agreed that the Lord (Yahweh) was the only true God and ultimate ruler of Israel, and that the Torah (the Law, found in the first five books of the Old Testament) was at the heart of their religion. But there were many opinions on just how their faith was to be put into practice.

At least four main strands can be identified, though we should note that there was great diversity even within them. And in any case the great majority of ordinary people belonged to no special group, though they probably found themselves in sympathy with one or another.

a. The Pharisees

The Pharisees were certainly influential, but numerically they were a small minority. Their aim was to keep the Law in every detail and maintain the purity of their faith, and to that end they developed hundreds of rules which were supposed to apply the Law to everyday life. They believed that the soul was immortal and there would be a future resurrection of the body. They saw God's hand overruling in human affairs.

It was, however, their ethical teaching which most characterised the Pharisees' party. They were usually held in high esteem, and considered to be models of righteous living. Many of the scribes, the students and teachers of the Law who also functioned as judges, were Pharisees. The Roman occupation and the religious compromises of the Herod family were abhorrent to the Pharisees. They looked for God to intervene, but did not attempt to change things by political or military action; they simply got on with trying to fulfil the Law in their individual lives.

b. The Sadducees

Even fewer than the Pharisees, but exercising considerable political power, were the Sadducees. They were drawn for the most part from the high-priestly and wealthier land-owning families. They controlled Temple affairs and had the majority in the Jewish ruling council, the Sanhedrin.

Sadducees accepted only the first five books of the Old Testament (the Law as given through Moses) as authoritative, and refused to accept any belief in immortality, resurrection, future judgement, angels and demons or God's over-ruling in human history. For them, the here and now was everything. It therefore made sense to them to co-operate with the country's rulers, whether the Romans or the Herods, to get the best deal they could, rather than pin their hopes on some future salvation.

c. The Zealots

The Zealots shared the Pharisees' distress that Gentile overlords should demand of the Jews tribute and obedience that by rights belonged only to God, the true King of Israel. But they saw it as their duty to drive out the occupying power by force. They were founded by Judas the Galilean around the time of Jesus' birth (Acts 5:37). The Zealots strongly resisted the payment of taxes to Rome, regarding it as treason, and made life difficult for the Romans by continuous guerilla activity.

A more wide-spread Jewish revolt began in AD 66, with the wholehearted involvement of the Zealots, and the response of Rome was severe. In AD 70, after an horrendous siege, Jerusalem was captured and the Temple utterly destroyed. Fighting continued, but the Zealots' last stronghold, the city of Masada, was captured in AD 74 with great loss of life.

d. The Essenes

Yet another way of responding to the situation in Palestine was represented by various groups known as the Essenes. They sought to withdraw altogether from the corrupt world around them, while they waited for God to intervene decisively in human history. When that happened they alone would emerge as God's chosen people, and they would rule with the Messiah. Many groups lived as isolated communities in the desert, observing strict rules and finding support for their beliefs in elaborate and detailed interpretations of the Old Testament scriptures. Admission to

Masada, looking at the northern end and Herod's Palace.

membership was by ritual purification in water after a lengthy period of preparation, and fellowship was expressed in simple ceremonial meals. The discovery of the so-called Dead Sea Scrolls in caves at Qumran in 1947 has greatly added to our knowledge of this strand of Judaism.

Jesus therefore was born, grew up and ministered amongst a people struggling to make sense of their cherished faith in the context of a world infused with Greek ideas and dominated politically by the Roman Empire. They were longing for God to save his people and establish his kingdom, and many looked for a messiah to appear. But there was no consensus on what exactly such a salvation would mean nor on how the kingdom would come.

EXPLORING FURTHER

The best way to grasp the information given in this unit is to begin to use it. Here are some suggestions:

THE WORLD OF THE NEW TESTAMENT

Look at the map of the New Testament world on page 10. It covers parts of the Roman and Parthian empires in the first century. Now read the account of the people present in Jerusalem on the Day of Pentecost (Acts 2:5–11) and find these places on the map. How can you explain the presence of these people at a Jerusalem festival?

What features of our own age could assist the spread of the gospel?

THE ETHIOPIAN

Read Acts 8:26–29. How could a North African have known about the God of the Jews? What might have attracted him to worship this God? What circumstances made the journey to Jerusalem easier? How, without understanding Hebrew, was he able to read the Old Testament?

SAUL OF TARSUS

○ Saul (Hebrew name), latterly known as Paul (Greek name);
○ born of Aramaic-speaking Jewish parents, and brought up strictly in the traditions of Judaism;
○ spent childhood in Tarsus, a Greek-speaking sea-port and university town in Asia Minor;
○ university education in Jerusalem; member of the party of the Pharisees; excellent student and renowned for religious zeal and achievement;
○ Roman citizen.

How could such a background have helped Paul in his mission to take the gospel to the first-century world?

How has God been at work in your own background, preparing you to serve him in some way?

THE RIGHT TIME

'. . . when the right time finally came, God sent his own Son . . .' (Gal 4:4 [GNB])

God chose to send Jesus into human history at a particular time and in a particular place. Can you suggest ways in which the world had been made ready for the ministry of Jesus and the mission of the Church?

UNIT 2

Into all the World

ACTS – A CAREFUL INVESTIGATION

An excellent first step towards understanding any piece of writing is to ask what the author's purpose was in writing it. What did he or she intend to achieve? If we understand that, we are much more likely to grasp what the document seeks to communicate. It also saves us from reading into it concerns of our own which were not in the author's mind at all and making of it something it does not set out to be.

In attempting to discover *why* a document was written it is clearly a great advantage to know *who* wrote it and *for whom*. Knowing *when* it was written and something about the author or recipient can also provide helpful clues about the situation which prompted the writing of the document.

For all these reasons we will give some detailed attention to these matters.

At first sight questions of authorship, date and place of composition and purpose may seem a distraction from the message, but such considerations help us to grasp the content more fully and accurately. We do well to follow the example of the author of Luke's Gospel and Acts, who 'carefully investigated everything from the beginning' (Luke 1:13). Clearly the inspiration of the Holy Spirit, of whom this author writes so much, does not rule out the demand for hard work!

TO THINK ABOUT . . .

How do you respond to Christians who tell you that they do not need to study; the Bible is all they need and the Holy Spirit will teach them all things?

WHO WROTE ACTS?

Acts 1:1 tells us that Luke and Acts were written by the same author. They are addressed to the same person and the style and language of the two books are identical. No author's name appears in either book, but it is clear that the writer of Acts was with the apostle Paul at certain times: in chapter 16 there is an abrupt change from speaking of Paul and his companions and what *they* did (*vv*.6–8) to *we* and *us* (*vv*.10–17). Further 'we' passages are found in 20:5–15; 21:1–18; 27:1–28:16.

Once those companions of Paul who are mentioned by name in Acts are eliminated, there are strong reasons for identifying Luke as the author. From Paul's letters we find that Luke was a fellow-worker (Phm 24) and faithful com-

panion who stuck with Paul even when others did not (2 Tim 4:9–11). He would have had ample opportunity on these journeys to obtain information from key figures in the story of the Church. Paul refers to him as 'our dear friend Luke, the doctor' (Col 4:14). The language and style of Luke and Acts show that they were written by a well-educated person. There are also precise medical descriptions which, while not proving that the author was a doctor, show that he was familiar with such terms.

The earliest surviving Christian writings which refer to Luke and Acts come from the second century AD and name Paul's companion Luke as the author.

We know little about Luke's background. There are grounds for believing that he was converted in Antioch when the gospel was first preached there to the Gentiles, but we cannot be sure. He joined Paul at Troas (Acts 16:9–11) and crossed with him into Macedonia, remaining for some time as pastor of the first church planted on the mainland of Europe, at Philippi. He is the only non-Jew whose writings are found in the New Testament.

TO WHOM WAS ACTS WRITTEN?

Both Luke and Acts are addressed to Theophilus (Luke 1:3; Acts 1:1). It is a Greek name which means 'one who loves God'. Although it is possible that Luke intended this as a general term to include all who love God, it is more likely that Theophilus was an actual individual.

The title 'most excellent' (Luke 1:3) was afforded to high-ranking Roman officials, and the language of Luke 1:1–4 suggests that Theophilus had been instructed in the Christian faith and that Luke hoped to strengthen that faith. Yet it is clear from the contents of the books that Luke intended them to reach a wider audience. Perhaps Theophilus was a wealthy patron who would ensure that they were copied and distributed.

WHEN WAS ACTS WRITTEN?

It is not easy to date New Testament books very precisely, and for most of them a wide range of possible dates has been suggested. Acts is no exception. From the contents it must have been completed after Paul arrived in Rome (c. AD 61). It is generally believed that Paul was martyred during the emperor Nero's persecution of AD 66/67. Luke does not mention this which suggests that Acts was finished before it took place. That depends, however, on what his purpose was in writing. Did he intend to give a full account of Paul's work, or was the final statement about Paul evangelising unhindered in Rome (Acts 28:31) the conclusion Luke would have chosen, even if he did know what happened later?

How does Acts relate to other New Testament writings? It was clearly written after Luke's Gospel (Acts 1:1). Also, since Luke used Mark's Gospel as source material, he was writing later than Mark, although dating of Mark is uncertain. There is no mention of Paul's letters in Acts, so Luke may have been writing at least before Paul's letters were widely circulated.

What we can say with confidence is that Luke probably collected material over a period, which he then carefully worked into its present form not long after events described in the book.

WHAT WAS LUKE'S PURPOSE?

Was Luke an **historian**, setting out to record the first thirty years of the Church's life? Did he write as a **theologian** to put across a particular understanding of the Christian faith? Or was he an **apologist**, not 'apologising' for something but presenting an 'apologia' or defence of the faith? Let us consider each possibility in turn.

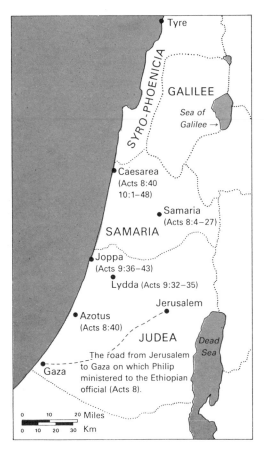

The map shows places mentioned in the early chapters of Acts as the gospel was proclaimed in 'Jerusalem, Judea and Samaria . . .'

LUKE THE HISTORIAN

Acts is the work of someone who took great care over details. When he refers to Roman officials, for example, he uses accurate terms for different places: there are 'anthypatoi' (pro-consuls) in Cyprus and Achaia (13:7–8; 18:12); 'strategoi' (magistrates) in Philippi (16:22); and 'politarchai' (city officials) in Thessalonica (17:8). Some of the terms were so little known that in the past some scholars have concluded that Luke must have been mistaken, but archaeological finds have proved him right!

Luke employs two techniques of the ancient historian. First, not only the terms but even the style and language of Luke's narrative are appropriate to the various places where the action takes place. Second, Luke uses speeches to good effect. These were not intended to be word for word reports, but rather to give the gist of what was said. One suspects, for example, that Peter and Paul preached for rather longer than it takes to read the accounts of their sermons in 3:14–39; 17:22–31; etc. It says much for Luke's integrity as an historian that, though he was writing thirty years after the earliest events he describes, the speeches show no trace of the phraseology and ideas which were current at a later date. His claim to have carefully researched and presented his information can be upheld.

If, however, Luke's aim was simply to recount the story of the Church's early life, his History leaves many gaps. We read a great deal about Peter and Paul, but what of the other apostles? Missionary work in certain areas is described in detail, but there is nothing about evangelism in North Africa or India where, according to tradition, the gospel was also preached. Paul's journey to Rome occupies an important place in Luke's account, but he does not tell us how the church in Rome, which was there before Paul arrived (28:15), was planted.

Luke writes with the care and instinct of an historian, but Acts must be both more and less than a record of the life and mission of the early church.

LUKE THE THEOLOGIAN

One dictionary defines theology as, 'The science treating of God, his nature and attributes, and his relation to man and the universe.' When we describe someone as a 'theologian' we mean that he or she is concerned to know and understand God and his dealings with the world. On that basis we can without hesitation call Luke a theologian.

One way we see this is by noting what he devotes space to. An historian dealing with his own day and age is aware of so much that is happening and so many people who can be drawn on for information, that it is a challenge to select what should go into his account. Luke the historian must have agonised over many incidents and personalities which he would have liked to include, but space was limited. What he has included is, then, an indication of what he considered important.

Reading Acts with this in mind, we find that Luke was deeply interested in several theological themes. Acts tells the story of the unfolding mission of the Church, taking the message of salvation to Jew, Samaritan and Gentile and ever further afield, and it does so in a profoundly theological way, demonstrating that this development was both God's intention and God's doing. Evangelistic sermons are recorded – his readers must be in no doubt as to the apostle's message. The activity of the Holy Spirit is high-lighted at many crucial points. Accounts are given of conversions to the Christian faith. The progress, in spite of opposition, of the word of God, the Church and individual Christians is described. The life and, to some extent, the organisation of the early church is portrayed.

So Luke certainly wrote with a theologian's interests and insights, but there is yet another dimension to his work.

LUKE THE APOLOGIST

It has sometimes been suggested that Luke's main aim was to argue for Christianity when it came under attack in the Roman Empire. He wanted to show that Christianity was no threat to the state, and that the church and her leaders could get on well with the Roman authorities. The Jewish religion was officially permitted and protected in the Roman Empire, and Luke was concerned to portray Christianity as a development within Judaism, deserving the same privileges. Perhaps Theophilus was actually Paul's lawyer when he went on trial before Caesar in Rome, and Acts was written as the defence brief! Another view is that Luke wrote to support Paul and his apostleship against critics and detractors on the Jewish wing of the Church.

Such an approach has two weaknesses. Whatever Luke is said to be defending, much of the material in Acts is superfluous to the case being presented; and some of this material could just as well be exploited by the opposition. If he is primarily an apologist, either for Christianity in the Empire or for Paul in the Church, he says too much!

Nonetheless, Luke will have been well aware of these and other current issues while he was writing, and where charges could be answered through the narrative and speeches which he records he will have taken that opportunity.

CONCLUSION

So what was Luke really setting out to accomplish? Probably all three of the suggestions we have looked at contain some truth. They are not incompatible.

The idea that someone writing from a theological standpoint cannot be relied upon as an historian stems from a nineteenth-century notion of what 'real history' should be. It does not stand up to examination. Even the person who sets out simply to record what happened, not attempting to interpret it in any way, cannot produce an absolutely objective account.

TO THINK ABOUT . . .

What would you write if you had to produce a one-page account of your church over the last year.

What would you include – or leave out? What or whom would you draw on for information? Both of these choices involve making judgements about what is important and significant.

Would you write about special events, regular church life, membership numbers, money, preaching themes, worship style, buildings?

Are your sources statistical returns, your own perceptions, interviews with leaders or others, comments from the local community, church magazines, minutes of meetings, or what?

Your one-page history will tell the discerning reader not only about your church but also about you and your understanding of what a church is and of what matters in its life.

We do not assume that in a trial any witness called by the defence must be lying in order to help out the defendant. Nor should we assume that if Luke consciously makes a defence he must therefore be fabricating or distorting the evidence. If the evidence itself answers the charges, then the witness has done his job by telling the truth.

It is perfectly possible, then, for a writer to be both a trustworthy historian and a perceptive theologian, and also speak at times as a witness for the defence.

LUKE'S OWN STATEMENT OF PURPOSE

When we consider how Luke himself sets out his aims, we find evidence of each of the three possibilities discussed above. To discover this we turn not to his second volume, Acts, but to the opening paragraph of his first volume, in Luke's Gospel 1:1–4.

A RELIABLE RECORD

Here he tells us that there have already been many accounts written of his subject (*v*.1). Why should he want to write another? The implication is that there are some inaccurate and disorderly accounts going about, and Luke means to correct and improve upon them, both by the care and accuracy of his investigation and by the clear, orderly manner in which he presents the information (*v*.3). This is Luke the historian speaking, determined to get at what really happened; he went to 'eye-witnesses' (*v*.2) and investigated his subject 'from the beginning' (*v*.3).

GOD'S PURPOSES UNFOLDED

But in the way he speaks of his subject, we see that he views in a special way the events which he is going to relate. They didn't just happen: they are 'the things that have been fulfilled among us' (*v*.1). This theme is carried through both Luke and Acts. In Jesus and in the Church, God's promises given to his people in the Old Testament are fulfilled. Luke and Acts together constitute the history of the accomplishment of God's purposes, and the unfolding of this theme governs Luke's choice of what to include and the order in which the story is told.

For this reason Luke refers to his sources as not only eye-witnesses but also servants of the word. It is in God's word in the Old Testament that he looks for an understanding of the events described. Moreover the account of Jesus and the Church is a continuation of the Old Testament story. Luke speaks of things that were 'handed down' (*v*.2) and 'taught' (*v*.4), terms which were used of the passing on of religious teaching. When he begins to tell the new part of the story, he abandons the classical Greek of these first four verses and adopts a style of Greek similar to that of the Greek translation of the Old Testament which Luke himself would have used. Rather in the manner of the Old Testament historian who wrote 1 and 2 Chronicles, Luke sets out to relate sacred history, describing real events, seeing in them God's activity, and drawing lessons for the people of God from what he relates.

A PRACTICAL PURPOSE

This practical purpose is also indicated in Luke's introduction. He is writing for Theophilus, 'so that you may know the certainty of the things you have been taught' (*v*.4). Theophilus and other readers are to be strengthened in their faith through this carefully researched account of the historical events upon which that faith is founded.

Luke's great theme of the accomplishment of God's purpose had, however, a particular application to such as Theophilus. The people of God in the Old Testament were Jews. Jesus and his apostles were Jews. The Church was born in Jerusalem. In the first decades of the Church's life there were those who questioned whether Gentiles such as Theophilus could really be part of God's people and regard God's promise of salvation as applying to them.

In answer to that Luke shows us that the coming of salvation to the Gentiles was God's own doing. It was his purpose from the beginning. Although in Acts we see the Church engaged in mission, it is God who by his Spirit has to push them out, initiating every advance and confirming every development. Theophilus and all other Gentile Christians may indeed have certainty; God himself has brought them salvation in Christ, and they are included in God's people.

A JOURNEY THROUGH ACTS

Acts is the longest book in the New Testament, and there are many ways of dividing it up.

Read the book through in a modern translation, with the help of the following outline. Do not get bogged down in the details, but try to grasp the story and the main points which Luke wants his readers to notice.

Reading with a map open before you will help. As you note where the action is taking place you will see that the geography of the book carries the theme forward. Luke's Gospel moves dramatically *towards* Jerusalem. In Acts the movement is *out from* Jerusalem, first into the surrounding regions, then to Asia Minor, on to the mainland of Europe, and culminating in the capital of the Empire and the centre of the Gentile world, Rome.

Three times in the book there is a statement that 'the word of God increased' (6:7; 12:24; 19:20). This gives an indication of how Luke has organised his material. The first section shows how the word of God increased in Jerusalem and leads up to the summary statement in 6:7. The second block of material begins with events in Jerusalem, concerning Stephen, but this is preparing for the thrust of the gospel out of Jerusalem into Samaria and other surrounding regions which is summarised in 12:24. The third section takes the story still further afield, leading up to the summary in 19:20.

From then on it is not so much the story of the mission which is narrated, but Paul's compulsion to go to Jerusalem and his journey from there to Rome. What the Lord told Ananias about Paul, that he would 'carry my name before the Gentiles and their kings and before the people of Israel' (9:15), is shown to have taken place, and in the process Paul bears witness in 'Jerusalem, Judea and Samaria' (Caesarea) and 'to the ends of the earth' (Rome). Luke's narrative concludes; the gospel has been rejected by Jews but has been preached freely at the very heart of the Gentile world.

INTRODUCTION (1:1–11)

The Ascension of Jesus is the hinge which joins Luke's first volume (the Gospel of Luke) to his second (Acts) (cf. Luke 24:50–52). The Gospel leads up to it; everything in Acts flows out of it. Jesus has proved that he is alive, and the Church's mission is essentially to witness to him and his kingdom. They will receive power for this task, whose scope is much vaster than any of them have imagined and which will continue until Jesus returns as King.

'IN JERUSALEM' (1:12–6:7)

a. The believers choose a replacement for Judas (1:12–26)

b. Pentecost (2:1–47)

○ The believers filled with the Holy Spirit (2:1–4).
○ People from all over the world hear in their own languages (2:5–13).
○ Peter's sermon and its effect (2:14–41).
○ Life in the community of believers (2:42–47).

c. A healing and its repercussions (3:1–4:31)

○ A crippled man healed (3:1–10).
○ Peter's sermon (3:11–26)
○ Opposition from the religious authorities (4:1–22).
○ The believers' prayer (4:23–31).

d. The sharing of possessions in the community of believers (4:32–5:11)

○ The pattern (4:32–35).
○ The example of Barnabas (4:36–37).
○ The sin of Ananias and Sapphira (5:1–11).

e. Signs and wonders and their effects (5:12–42)

○ Many believe and many come for healing (5:12–16).
○ Opposition from the high priest and his party (5:17–40).
○ The apostles' response to persecution (5:41–42).

f. A problem of growth dealt with (6:1–6)

● Summary: so the word of God spread (6:7).

e. The Gospel in Antioch (11:19–30)

○ The Gospel preached to Gentiles (11:19–21).
○ Barnabas sent to evaluate (11:22–24).
○ Barnabas finds Saul (11:25–26).
○ The church sends help to Judea (11:27–30).

f. Herod persecutes the church (12:1–23)

○ Peter's imprisonment and escape (12:1–19).
○ Herod's pride and end (12:19–23).

● Summary: the word of God continued to increase (12:24)

'IN ALL JUDEA AND SAMARIA' (6:8–12:24)

a. Stephen (6:8–8:1)

○ Stephen's ministry and the opposition he faced (6:8–15).
○ Stephen's speech to the Sanhedrin (7:1–53).
○ Stephen's death (7:54–8:1).
○ The church persecuted and scattered (8:1–3).

b. Philip (8:4–40)

○ Philip's ministry in Samaria (8:4–8).
○ Simon the Sorcerer (8:9–25).
○ Philip and the Ethiopian (8:26–40).

c. Saul (9:1–31)

○ Conversion and commission (9:1–19).
○ Witness in Damascus (9:19–25).
○ In Jerusalem (9:26–30).

● Summary: the church throughout Judea, Galilee and Samaria . . . grew (9:31)

d. Peter (9:32–11:18)

○ Ministry in Lydda (9:32–35).
○ Ministry in Joppa (9:36–43).
○ Ministry to the household of Cornelius (10:1–48).
○ The 'Gentile question' discussed in Jerusalem (11:1–18).

TO THE ENDS OF THE EARTH (12:25–19:20)

a. From Antioch as far as Galatia (12:25–14:28)

○ The church at Antioch sends out Barnabas and Saul (12:25–13:3).
○ On Cyprus (13:4–12).
○ In Pisidian Antioch (13:13–52).
○ In Iconium (14:1–7).
○ In Lystra (14:8–20).
○ In Derbe (14:21a).
○ Revisiting the new church (14:21b–25).
○ Back in Antioch (14:26–28).

b. The 'Gentile question' (15:1–35)

○ Paul and Barnabas sent to Jerusalem (15:1–4).
○ Discussion amongst church leaders (15:5–21).
○ Letter to Gentile believers (15:22–35).

c. From Antioch as far as Greece (15:36–18:23)

○ Paul and Barnabas part company (15:36–41).
○ Timothy joins Paul (16:1–5).

● Summary: so the churches . . . grew (16:5)

○ Guidance to go to Macedonia (16:6–10).
○ In Philippi (16:11–40).
○ In Thessalonica (17:1–9).

○ In Berea (17:10–15).
○ In Athens (17:16–33).
○ In Corinth (18:1–17).
○ Back to Antioch via Ephesus (18:18–22).
○ Paul in Antioch, Galatia and Phrygia (18:23).

The Parthenon in Athens, a stone's throw from where Paul delivered his speech to the 'Men of Athens' (Acts 17). The Parthenon, or Temple of Athena, was regarded primarily as an artistic masterpiece and as the state treasury, but was also full of 'objects of worship'.

Photograph by Derek James

d. In Ephesus and into Asia (18:24–19:20)

○ Apollos (18:24–28).
○ Paul's ministry in Ephesus (19:1–19).
● Summary: the word of the Lord spread (19:20)

TO JERUSALEM, AND THEN TO ROME (19:21–28:31)

a. On the way to Jerusalem (19:21–21:16)

○ Paul's plan (19: 21–22).
○ The riot in Ephesus (19:23–41).
○ Paul's travels (20:1–6).
○ A long sermon at Troas (20:7–12).
○ Paul hurries on (20:13–16).
○ Farewell to the Ephesian elders (20:17–38).
○ Travelling on to Jerusalem (21:1–16).

b. In Jerusalem (21:17–23:22)

○ Paul and the Jewish believers (21:17–26).
○ Trouble in the temple (21:27–36).
○ Paul's defence before the crowd (21:37–22:21).
○ Paul invokes his citizenship (22:22–29).
○ Paul before the Sanhedrin (22:30–23:10).
○ Paul encouraged by a vision (22:11).

c. On to Caesarea (23:12–35)

○ A plot to kill Paul (22:12–22).
○ Paul escorted to Caesarea (23:23–35).

d. In Caesarea (24:1–26:32)

○ Paul's trial before Felix (24:1–27).
○ Paul's trial before Festus (25:1–12).
○ Festus discusses Paul's case with King Agrippa (25:13–22).
○ Paul's case investigated by King Agrippa (25:23–26:32).

e. Journey to Rome (27:1–28:15)

○ A difficult voyage (27:1–12).
○ Shipwrecked (27:13–44).
○ On Malta (28:1–10).
○ The final stage of the journey (28:11–15).

f. In Rome (28:16–31)

The harbour at Caesarea from where Paul set sail on his journey to Rome.

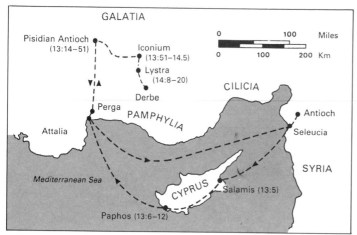

Paul's First Journey (Acts 13:1–14:28)

EXPLORING FURTHER

Having journeyed through Acts, return to explore more fully some particular themes. Consider one or more of the following:

THE HOLY SPIRIT

In what ways does the Holy Spirit carry forward the mission of the Church in the book of Acts?

PREACHING THE GOOD NEWS

Luke records a number of sermons to various groups of people (e.g. 2:14–41; 3:11–26; 10:34–46; 13:16–48; 17:22–34). From these consider:

a. what is the content of the gospel which these early Christians proclaimed?

b. how does the presentation of the gospel vary according to the audience?

Think of a group of people that you know. How could you communicate that same content to them? What degree of understanding and knowledge could you assume? What starting point might they relate to which could lead into a presentation of the good news of Jesus?

MISSION STRATEGY

What can be discovered in Acts about how Paul brought the gospel to a new region? In each city, to whom did he go first, and why? What did he do with those who became Christians?

Can you apply any of this to a mission strategy for your neighbourhood?

LIFE IN THE COMMUNITY OF BELIEVERS

From the information which Luke gives, describe life both in the Jerusalem church before it was scattered and in the church at Antioch. Which of these features should be evident in every church?

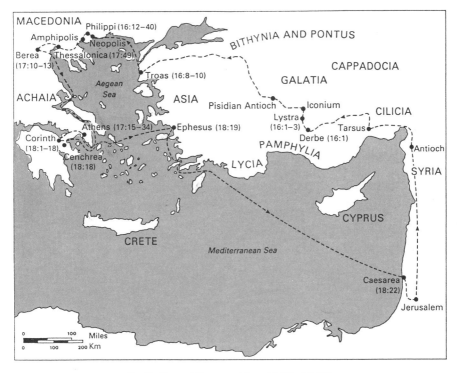

Paul's Second Journey (Acts 15:36–18:22)

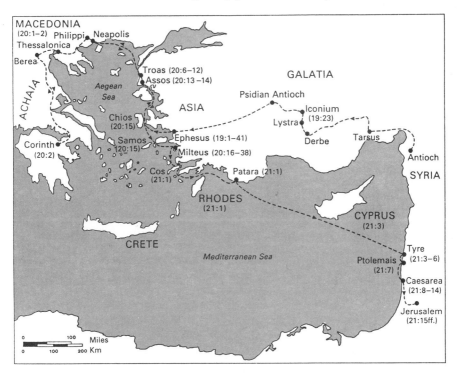

Paul's Third Journey (Acts 18:23–21:17)

UNIT 3

Paul and his First Letters

Do you realise how much God used one man in the early spread of the gospel and the development of the Church? Accounts of Paul's work take up a good proportion of the book of Acts, and two-thirds of the New Testament letters derive from him.

Paul's appearance, however, was not particularly impressive, if we can believe the second-century writer of *The Acts of Paul and Thecla*:

> . . . a man little of stature, thin-haired upon the head, crooked in the legs, of good state of body, with eyebrows joining, and nose somewhat hooked, full of grace: for sometimes he appeared like a man, and sometimes he had the face of an angel.

He must have been fit, to endure the travelling and other hardships of which we read. And, to judge from the knowledge of Christ to which his letters testify, at times he must have carried a radiance from the presence of God. To these impressions we can add an outline of Paul's life from his letters and from the book of Acts.

PAUL'S LIFE

A PRIVILEGED HOME

Like most first-century Jews, Paul, or Saul as he was named, was born outside Palestine. His home was Tarsus, a thriving city of half a million inhabitants on the coast of Cilicia. His family had important contacts in Jerusalem, and the young Saul was brought up strictly in the traditions of the Pharisees. His parents also enjoyed the coveted privilege of Roman citizenship, which therefore passed to Saul by right of birth.

At the port of Tarsus, Saul would have seen and heard merchants from all over the world, and the city's famous university was a centre for the ideas of Greek philosophers and poets. From birth, Saul inhabited the two worlds of traditional Judaism and the Roman structures and hellenistic culture of the international community.

MAKING HIS MARK

To continue his education Saul was sent to Jerusalem where he studied under Gamaliel, the foremost Jewish teacher of his day. Saul showed exceptional ability as a student and great re-

ligious zeal. At a younger age than usual he became a council member (which may imply either of a synagogue or of the Sanhedrin) and used his vote against the Christians. He was present and gave his approval when the first execution of a Christian, Stephen, took place. Not content with that, he sought and was given official authority to direct the persecution.

STOPPED IN HIS TRACKS

In pursuit of Christians who had taken refuge in Damascus, the capital of Syria, Saul was suddenly thrown to the ground by a dazzling light and a voice from heaven. Saul realised that the risen Lord Jesus Christ had appeared to him, and he was led blinded and stunned into the city where he remained neither eating nor drinking for three days. Eventually the godly but timorous Ananias visited him to pray for him, baptise him and welcome him as a fellow Christian. Saul's life had taken a complete U-turn. From that point on he was utterly dedicated to knowing and serving the one whose followers he had previously sought to destroy.

Straight Street (still called by that name) in Damascus where, following his conversion, Paul lodged in the house of Judas.

SAUL THE CHRISTIAN

Having been commissioned by Jesus to preach the gospel, Saul began straight away in Damascus. Apart from a brief period in the surrounding desert, Saul remained there for three years. He gained the trust and love of the Christians in Damascus but also incurred the resentment of the Jews.

It was this growing opposition which compelled him to leave Damascus and flee to Jerusalem. There Barnabas took him under his wing and introduced him to a still understandably suspicious Jerusalem church. His stay in Jerusalem was short, because again he met opposition from certain Jews.

He returned via Capernaum to his native city of Tarsus, and of the ten years he spent there we are told nothing. But we can reasonably surmise that as at Damascus he preached and taught and continued to study the Old Testament scriptures which he had known since childhood. But in those scriptures he now saw Jesus as the promised Messiah, discerned God's way of making

people right with himself through faith, and grasped the world-wide extent of God's salvation.

TEACHING THE CHURCH AT ANTIOCH

A significant step forward in the history of the Church took place when some Christians, driven out of Jerusalem by the persecution, went to the important city of Antioch in Syria (the third largest city in the Empire) and began to preach the gospel not only to Jews but also to the Gentiles. A church was formed, the first to consist of people who had come to Christ from totally outside the Jewish faith.

The Jerusalem leaders sent Barnabas to investigate, and he rejoiced to see that this was indeed God's doing. He stayed on to encourage them and help in evangelism, but he also saw the need to teach the new church. Who better for that task than Saul, familiar with the Hellenistic world, trained in Judaism as a teacher of the Scriptures, and now called by the Lord to bring the light of salvation to the Gentiles? Barnabas sought him out in Tarsus and brought him the 120 miles to Antioch. There they worked together for a year, exercising a teaching ministry, and then returned together to Jerusalem, taking a gift from the new Christians to relieve the distress of their fellow-believers in Judea at a time of famine.

TO THINK ABOUT . . .

Antioch was an important city in the Roman Empire and the capital of the province of Syria. If Christianity could take hold in such strategic centres, it stood a greater chance of spreading rapidly through the network of roads and trade routes.

So the early Christians sought to establish strong congregations in these strategic centres. What lessons could Christians today learn from this practice which could be applied to plans and strategies for church planting?

SENT OUT IN MISSION

Having benefited from the ministry of Barnabas and Saul, the Antioch church was willing to commission them, at God's command, for the work of mission. Thus was Saul launched upon a missionary life of breathtaking scope. At their first port of call, Barnabas's native island of Cyprus, it was Saul who emerged as leader.

From this point in Luke's narrative the Hebrew name 'Saul' ('asked [of God]') is replaced by the Greek 'Paul' ('small'). Though he never forgot his own people, the focus of Paul's mission was the Gentile world, and perhaps the change of name indicated a willingness to adapt and identify himself with those to whom he was to go.

From Cyprus the missionaries journeyed through Southern Galatia, and from there returned to report back to the sending church at Antioch.

A NETTLE TO GRASP

How far should Gentiles who became Christians be required to observe the ceremonial laws of Judaism? There were those, especially in Jerusalem, who thought that by not making these demands of the new Gentile Christians Paul and Barnabas were compromising on essentials. Some holding such views had gone among the new Gentile churches in Galatia trying to persuade these recent converts to accept circumcision and Jewish dietary laws.

Paul wrote a strong letter to the Galatian churches (see page 56) insisting that Christ had set them free and they were saved by faith, and must on no account submit to such pressure. Then, again with Barnabas, he visited Jerusalem to participate in a Council of the Church called to resolve this problem. They were glad to return to Antioch with a sympathetic and encouraging message from the Jerusalem Christians, and for a time they resumed their ministry in Antioch itself.

BREAKTHROUGH INTO EUROPE

Paul's next trip was in the company of Silas. He had disagreed with Barnabas over whether or not to take with them John Mark, who had set off with them before but had not stayed the course. After visiting the new churches Paul was planning to advance westward into Asia, but the Lord closed that door and pointed him in another direction through a vision of a man from Macedonia asking for help. Thus Paul and his team entered the European mainland, and churches were planted from Philippi through to Athens and Corinth.

Paul remained in Corinth for two years, but continued to teach and encourage the new churches of Macedonia through his colleagues, Silas and Timothy, and the two letters to the Thessalonians.

ESTABLISHING THE WORK IN ASIA

On the way back from Corinth to Jerusalem and Antioch, Paul took the opportunity to make an initial visit to Asia. He landed in Ephesus where he made contact with the Jewish community and left a Christian couple to set up home there when he continued his journey.

After some time back in Antioch Paul set out again but this time, though he visited churches on the way, it was not so much a missionary tour as a move to a new base, Ephesus. From this city, the commercial capital of Asia, the gospel spread out into the surrounding region, and Paul was also able to make evangelistic and pastoral trips. He kept in close touch with the church in Corinth by letter and eventually by a personal visit.

ON TO ROME

The apostle, however, still looked further afield. He believed that the Lord intended him to preach the gospel in Rome, right at the political heart of the first-century world, and he had hopes of travelling beyond Rome to Spain. His letter to the group of Christians which already existed in Rome, written during that last visit to Corinth, indicates his plans (Romans 15:23–33).

Paul did reach Rome, but not as a free traveller. Fully aware of the danger involved, he had gone to Jerusalem, eager to bring to the church there a collection for the needy that he had organised amongst the Gentile churches. He soon met violent opposition and spent time in custody, first in Jerusalem and then in Caesarea before, having claimed his right as a Roman citizen to be tried before Caesar himself, he was escorted to the capital as a prisoner.

Here the book of Acts leaves him. As we noticed earlier, Luke intended his readers to see significance in the geographical scheme of the book, beginning in Jerusalem and concluding with the gospel being openly proclaimed in Rome. Though it was an appropriate point to close the book of Acts, we are left wondering what happened to Paul subsequently. Some early Christian writers, such as Clement, mention a visit of Paul to Spain, and some scholars find a later period of ministry to be the most convincing setting for the letters 1 Timothy and Titus (see p.78). 2 Timothy suggests another, more severe imprisonment in Rome under the threat of death, and there is a strong tradition that Paul was executed during a period of persecution by Emperor Nero (AD 67).

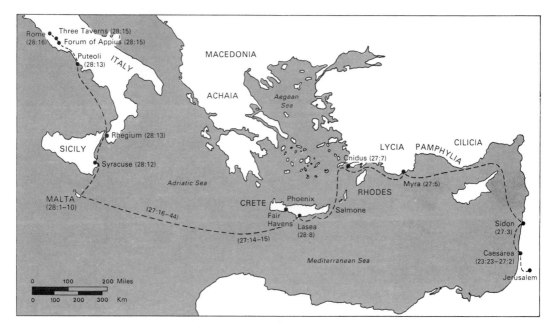

Paul's Journey to Rome (Acts 27:1–28:16)

PAUL'S MINISTRY

Paul was by any standard a remarkable man. He was a marvellously effective **pioneer missionary**, with great courage, physical resilience, strength of resolve, intellectual ability and a sympathetic understanding of people with widely differing cultures and beliefs. He developed clear strategies, while remaining sensitive to the guidance of the Holy Spirit, who at times overruled Paul's plans. He was able to lead, train and mobilise others.

His letters reveal the heart of a **pastor**, aching with concern for those churches and individuals which were under threat, and brimming over with love and joy as he prayed for the ever-increasing band of brothers and sisters in Christ throughout the world.

Many think of him as primarily a **theologian**. This he certainly was, but not in the sense of someone concerned with philosophical speculation as an end in itself. The theological thinking that we find in Paul's letters is immensely practical, seeking to understand and apply the gospel and often to find answers to specific issues which had arisen in the life of a church.

In his missionary preaching and teaching he was able to utilise some of the philosophical ideas of his day, but it would be misleading to portray him as the originator of a 'Greek' type of Christianity opposed to the 'Jewish' Christianity taught by Jesus. Paul's sources were the Old Testament scriptures, which he used in the manner of a Jewish rabbi; the teaching of Jesus; the gospel events themselves; and the knowledge of God that came through his own communion with Christ.

Above all else, he was a **'man in Christ'**. The letters allow us to glimpse something of his own spiritual experience, the radical transformation which his conversion effected, his longings, strivings, joys and breathtaking insights.

The statue of the Apostle Paul which looks out across the sea from St Paul's island in Malta.

> ### TO THINK ABOUT . . .
> Look back to the item on Saul of Tarsus in the 'Exploring Further' section on page 19. You may want to pause now and reflect further on the questions asked in that section.

PAUL'S LETTERS

Half of the twenty-six documents which make up the New Testament are letters attributed to Paul. Doubtless he wrote other letters in the course of his ministry which are not found in the New Testament, but those which are contained there have profoundly affected the content of Christian belief and the shape of church life through 2000 years. They continue as the focus of discussion for Christians in matters of faith and life as diverse as the doctrine of salvation, the role of women in the church, 'spiritual gifts', a Christian attitude to the government, and much more! As early as the time that Peter was writing his letters, some at least of Paul's letters were regarded as inspired writings on a level with the Old Testament scriptures (2 Pet 3:16).

From that 2 Peter reference we also see that even then not everything in Paul's letters was easy to understand, and some wanted to distort the meaning of them to their own advantage. We must read them, therefore, as carefully and honestly as possible, with the aim of letting them speak, rather than trying merely to use them to support our own opinions.

TO WHOM WAS EACH WRITTEN AND WHY?

The first rule in reading the New Testament letters is to remember that that is what they are! While they vary from the intensely personal, such as Paul's letter to his friend Philemon, to those which, like the letter to the Romans, read more like essays or sermons, **all were written as letters**.

This fact leads to two implications that we must take seriously if we are going to understand Paul's letters: he wrote to actual people in specific situations, and he had a purpose in writing to those people at that time.

a. Written to particular people.

We cannot simply assume that everything in the letters applies to other groups of people (such as ourselves) in the same way that Paul intended it to apply to those to whom he wrote. The fact that they are found in the New Testament is

evidence that from very early in its life the Church, guided by the Holy Spirit, has treasured these letters as God-inspired writings, true and relevant beyond the confines of their original destinations. Our responsibility is to discover, with the help of the same Holy Spirit, exactly how they apply to us.

The first step is to ask what Paul wanted to say to his original readers. We must then ask what he would say if he were writing to us, in our twentieth-century village, town or city. Where we find that the situation addressed in the letters is still familiar today, the teaching and guidance given by the apostle may be applied directly. Often, however, the particular problem dealt with may not trouble us, at least not in the same form, or the answers given may seem to relate much better to first-century culture than to our own. When this happens we must try to sift out the underlying principles valid for Christians in every age, from specific applications which were appropriate to particular situations in the world of the original readers but which may not make so much sense in our own context.

The more we know about the people to whom the letters were written, their circumstances and the ideas and attitudes of the culture in which they lived, the better we will understand the problems which the apostle was addressing, and how he applied the truths of the Christian faith to them. We will then be in a position to judge more accurately how the letters apply to us.

b. Written for a particular reason

As letters, they came into being not because Paul decided to sit down and write a pamphlet on some topic but because there was a situation which required his involvement. It could be that Paul became aware of some problem that had arisen in a church, or that his guidance was sought on some matter; perhaps news of a church's teaching or behaviour caused concern that the gospel was being misunderstood or distorted; or there might be some action that Paul wanted a particular church or individual to undertake. There was always a specific purpose in the writing of each letter.

The discovery of that purpose is crucial to the understanding of each letter. It enables us to see why the particular contents were included, and other equally important matters left out. It helps us to make sense of the letter's overall scheme, to see where the argument is going and how each part contributes to it.

As we read, we need to keep in mind those two questions, 'to whom was this written?' and 'why?'.

READ THEM AS LETTERS

Letters tend to have a set form (we shall look more closely at the standard form of first-century Greek letters when we examine 1 Thessalonians), and their contents usually make more sense when we start at the beginning and read them straight through! The original recipients would naturally have read or heard them in this way, and we should do the same. We must, of course, go on to consider parts of them in greater detail, but the first step should be to read a letter through, trying to see what the main point is and how the letter develops. Christians would be spared from many zany and off-beat interpretations if they remembered that individual phrases, sentences and verses must not be forced to make some sort of sense on their own if they were intended to form part of a larger statement or argument.

For that reason we must cultivate the habit of reading the letters in paragraphs rather than in verses, noticing when Paul moves on to a fresh subject or starts to make another point. Even the chapter divisions, though often helpful, can sometimes cut across the natural units of thought.

TO THINK ABOUT . . .
How do you respond to the points made in the preceding paragraphs? How will what you have learned affect your future reading of New Testament letters?

LETTERS TO THE THESSALONIANS

It is now time to put all this into practice. The letters which Paul wrote to the Christians at Thessalonica are a good place to start. They are possibly the earliest of Paul's New Testament letters and were written in response to particular needs. From Acts and the letters themselves we can glean quite a lot of information which will aid our understanding of those needs.

THESSALONICA

Thessalonica (modern Thessaloniki) was and is one of the most important cities in northern Greece. With 200 000 inhabitants it was the capital and largest city in its region. As a seaport at the junction of two important trade routes it was a major centre of commerce. The population was largely Greek, but it included a Jewish community.

PAUL'S CONTACT WITH THE THESSALONIANS

It was while on his second missionary journey that Paul had his vision of a 'man of Macedonia' calling him over to mainland Europe (Acts 16:9–10). Thessalonica was the second European city (Philippi had been the first) in which Paul and his companions preached in response to that call. There is an account of their experience in Acts 17:1–15, from which we can discover the following:

○ where Paul began to preach (*v*.2);
○ his message (*vv*.2–3);
○ what sort of people the first converts were (*v*.4);
○ the role of *a*. the Jews, *b*. the local thugs, *c*. the general population and *d*. the city officials in the opposition which arose (*vv*.5–9);

A view of modern Thessaloniki from the south walls of the Acropolis.

○ the accuracation against the missionaries and the new Christians (*vv*.6–7);
○ the general response of the Thessalonians, even though there were some converts, in contrast with that of the people of Berea (*v*.11);
○ evidence of the strength of the Thessalonian Jews' opposition to the Christians (*v*.13);
○ how long Paul and his team had in Thessalonica (*v*.2).

TO THINK ABOUT . . .

Paul therefore left behind a small group of new Christians, mainly Gentiles but including some Jews. He had had only a few weeks in which to teach them, and already they were being persecuted and misrepresented. Can you see what Paul would be anxious about, the longer he was separated from them?

The Acts account shows that Paul then went on to Athens. From there, because unable to go himself, he sent Timothy to Thessalonica to encourage the young church and report back to him (1 Thess 3:1–2). Paul had moved on to Corinth when Timothy found him again (Acts 18:5). On hearing Timothy's news Paul immediately wrote his first letter to the Thessalonian Christians (1 Thess 3:6). It was now AD 51, the time of Gallio's proconsulship (Acts 18:12), and probably about six months had elapsed since Paul's stay in Thesalonica. After a further six months, on receipt of more news, Paul sent the second letter.

1 THESSALONIANS

'may he strengthen your hearts'

BACKGROUND BRIEFING

TO THINK ABOUT . . .

Read through 1 Thessalonians. Don't get bogged down at this stage with detail but get an overview of the letter as a whole. Divide a sheet of paper into three sections, and as you read make brief notes on anything you discover about:

- the people to whom the letter was written;
- Paul's attitude towards them;
- any specific reasons for writing.

You may prefer to read the letter through quickly first without making notes, and then read it a second time looking for this information.

In reading the letter you may have noticed the following points.

THE LETTER'S RECIPIENTS

○ These were 'model' converts (1:7);

- their faith was evidenced by what they did (1:3);
- the Holy Spirit had clearly been at work in them (1:4–6);
- their faith was an example and witness to others (1:7–10);
- they had received the message as the word of God (2:13).

○ Paul and his colleagues had worked hard and effectively among them (2:1–12) but had then been separated from them (2:17–18).

○ They were being persecuted (3:3–4).

○ Despite this they were standing firm in the Lord (3:8).

○ They were already doing many of the things that Paul hoped to see in them (4:1,10–11; 5:11).

○ There were some matters on which they needed further teaching (4:13).

PAUL'S ATTITUDE TOWARDS THEM

○ He was thankful to God for them (1:2; 2:13; 3:9).

○ He loved them and took great joy in them (2:8,19).

○ He longed to see them, or at least to have news of them (2:17–18; 3:1–2,10–11).

○ He was worried in case the persecution would shake their faith (3:3,5).

SPECIFIC REASONS FOR WRITING

○ He had just received news of them from Timothy (3:6), and had been told that they longed to see him.

○ He wanted to reinforce instructions he had given them about how Christians should live (4:1).

○ There seemed to be anxiety about what happened to Christians who died before Jesus' return. Paul wanted to clear this up (4:13–18) and give more teaching about how to live in the light of Jesus' coming (5:1–11).

You may well have picked up other points on reading and re-reading the letter. If on the other hand you feel you missed a lot, don't worry! You may be acquiring a new skill, a fresh way of reading the New Testament, and it takes practice. We are already, however, gaining a better understanding of the recipients of this letter, the writer's relationship with them and the circumstances and concerns which prompted him to write.

A JOURNEY THROUGH 1 THESSALONIANS

The next step is to construct a working outline of the letter: we want to break it down into its main sections, giving us the route for our journey.

In this task we are helped by the fact that Greek letters written at that time tended to follow a set pattern:

Opening section

● address (from . . . to . . .);
● greeting;
● thanksgiving for the health of the person(s) the letter is addressed to;

Main content

Closing section

● personal news and greetings;
● farewell.

Many, though not all, of the New Testament letters follow this basic pattern. Where they do not, it is worth considering whether the writer has deliberately departed from the expected pattern in order to make a point.

TO THINK ABOUT . . .

Using the letter pattern set out above, see if you can identify those elements in Paul's first letter to the Thessalonians – there is no 'personal news' at the end, but you should be able to find everything else.

Paul follows the pattern in this letter, but he expands on the basic elements.

OPENING SECTION

a. Address (1:1)

Even the address provides Paul with the opportunity to make a theological point, describing those he is writing to as 'in God the Father and our Lord Jesus Christ'.

b. Greeting (1:1)

The usual Greek greeting was one word, 'chairein', meaning simply 'greetings'. For this Paul substitutes the similar word 'charis', 'grace', to make a specifically Christian greeting, adding 'and peace'.

c. Thanksgiving (1:2–2:16)

Clearly this is much more than a polite formality. A typical Greek letter would have had something like: 'I thank the gods that you are in good health.' But with Paul this becomes an outpouring of thanksgiving to God for these Thessalonian Christians and all God has done in them, which spills over into the main body of the letter. It could be equally valid to consider this section finishing either at 1:10, because 2:1 could be regarded as the start of the main content, or alternatively at 3:13, because he is giving thanks again at the end of chapter 3 (see *v*.9).

It just goes to show that the letter pattern is a useful guide, and can be very helpful in making sense of a letter, but it should not be regarded as an inflexible rule.

MAIN CONTENT (2:17–5:24)

We will return to this when considering the purpose of the letter.

CLOSING SECTION

a. Final greetings (5:25–27)

b. Farewell (5:28)

THE PURPOSE OF THE LETTER

Most of the sections we have isolated could be broken down into yet smaller units, but it is especially important to do this with the section that we have identified as the 'main content', because here we shall discover what the writer really wanted to communicate.

TO THINK ABOUT . . .

Look through the main content section again and break it into smaller sections: notice where there is a change of subject.

There are three main subject areas, a final group of various instructions, and a prayer:

○ Paul's longing to see the Thessalonians (2:17 3:13);
○ living to please God (4:1–11);
○ Jesus' coming again (4:12–5:11);
○ various instructions (5:12–22);
○ prayer (5:23–24).

TO THINK ABOUT . . .

Noting the three main subjects and taking into consideration the information we gathered about the Thessalonian church and Paul's own circumstances, what do you think was Paul's purpose in writing this letter? What did he hope it would achieve?

The subjects that the letter deals with fit well with what we know of the background. Combining the two, we can see what Paul was hoping to do.

a. To reassure

Paul had been forcibly separated from these young Christians: he wants to reassure them of his love, and show that it is not lack of desire or effort that has kept him away.

b. To reinforce

They were living in a pagan Greek city, and Paul wanted to reinforce the moral teaching that he had given them in the short time he had spent with them.

c. To explain

They had gladly accepted the truth of Christ's glorious return but were confused on some aspects of Paul's teaching on the subject. Paul therefore wanted to clear up their anxiety about Christians who died before Jesus' return. He also wanted to direct them away from fruitless speculation about the timing of the event into the practical implications of how Christians should live.

d. To encourage

We have noticed that Paul departs from the normal form of a Greek letter in expanding the 'thanksgiving' from a polite sentence or two into an extensive section detailing his gratitude to God for the Thessalonians. This indicates that he is eager to encourage these young Christians.

EXPLORING FURTHER

The work that we have already done has given us some awareness of the background to this letter, its writer and recipients, an overview of its contents and some understanding of its purpose. We are now in a much better position to examine specific themes or topics and individual sections of the letter. We will now be able to see them in the context of the whole.

Having worked on the letter, perhaps you have noticed matters that you wish to follow up. As you do so, read in paragraphs, asking constantly what point is being made, and how does each sentence contribute to it. The following are suggestions for more detailed study.

MODELS

In the Greek world the personal example of moral teachers was considered a vital part of their teaching. Pupils were encouraged to remember the way of life that they had seen in their teacher and imitate it. Alongside this teachers gave clear instructions on specific matters. Paul employs the same method with the Thessalonians.

○ Paul says that the Thessalonian Christians became 'imitators' of the apostle and his missionary team (1:6). What features of the life that Paul lived among them as evangelist and pastor, of which he reminds them in 2:1–12, were worthy of imitation by these young Christians?
○ The Thessalonian converts themselves became a 'model' to other believers (1:7). In what ways (see 1:2–10; 2:13–15)?

How important is example in both communicating the Christian faith and teaching new Christians today?

LIVING TO PLEASE GOD

It was clearly Paul's goal that his converts should live lives worthy of God (2:12, also 1:9). What are the characteristics of such a life, and what reasons does Paul give for living it (4:1–11; 5:12–24; see also 1:9–10; 3:12–13)?

JESUS' RETURN

The fact that Jesus was coming had obviously been part of Paul's teaching in the short time he had been in Thessalonica, and it seems that the Christians had seized on it with enthusiasm, but had misunderstood some aspects of the teaching.

a. Identify two specific concerns which had surfaced (4:13; 5:1).

b. What additional information does Paul give to help clear up each of these points (4:13–17; 5:1–3)?

c. How did his confidence that Jesus was coming affect Paul's own attitudes and goals, and how did he want it to affect the lives of the Thessalonians (5:4–11; see also 1:9–10; 2:19; 3:13; 4:18)?

2 THESSALONIANS

'stand firm and hold to the teachings'

BACKGROUND BRIEFING

Only a few months elapsed between the writing of the first and second letters to the Thessalonians. Possibly Timothy and Silas had returned from Thessalonica bringing news, to which Paul wished to respond. They therefore form part of the same 'conversation'.

> **TO THINK ABOUT . . .**
> Read through 2 Thessalonians, asking yourself the question, 'Why was this second letter necessary?' Can you find:
>
> - a subject dealt with in the first letter which Paul thought it necessary to explain further;
> - any reference to specific things which had happened which caused Paul concern?

You will observe that the subject of Jesus' return is again a major topic. Whereas in the first letter Paul was answering questions about what would happen to Christians who died before it took place, and about the timing of it, his concern here is different. Notice the reference he makes to 'some prophecy, report or letter supposed to have come from us, saying that the day of the Lord has already come' (2:2). It seems that some were introducing erroneous teaching and seeking credibility for it by claiming that it had come from Paul himself. The apostle had to persuade them that Jesus' return was still in the future. He also had to take pains to demonstrate that this letter was genuienly from him (3:17).

There is another clue to Paul's motivation for writing in the comment, 'We hear that some among you are idle' (3:11). There were those

who had abandoned their everyday work and responsibilities, so convinced were they that Jesus was either just about to return or indeed had done so already. Paul wanted them to be in readiness for that event, but to live responsibly while they waited.

Perhaps the severe persecution these Christians were undergoing (1:4; see also 1 Thess 1:6; 2:14; 3:3) made them particularly eager for the coming of Jesus as King to release them from suffering. They were by no means the last group in the history of the Church who, struggling with intense affliction locally, have imagined that these must surely be the troubles that were predicted for the end time.

The remains of the great triumphal arch of Galerius in Thessaloniki.

Photograph by W.C.R. Hancock

A JOURNEY THROUGH 2 THESSALONIANS

OPENING SECTION

a. Address (1.1)

b. Greeting (1.2)

c. Thanksgiving (1:3–12)

Paul's thanksgiving flows into comment on what will be the main subject of the letter, the return of Jesus (1:8–10). This in turn leads into prayer (1:11–12).

MAIN CONTENT (2:1–3:15)

a. The lawlessness which will precede the coming of Jesus (2:1–12)

Paul speaks not only of a general resistance to God's rule but of the focus of that rebellion in 'the man of lawlessness'. This term is found nowhere else in the New Testament, though certain characteristics of this figure are similar to those of the 'antichrist' in, for example, Revelation 13.

b. Confidence that they will stand firm (2:13–3:5)

c. Warning against idleness (3:6–15)

CLOSING SECTION

a. Final greeting (3:16–17)

Paul needs to emphasise the authenticity of this letter (see 2:2).

b. Farewell (3:18)

EXPLORING FURTHER

BLESSING IN AFFLICTION

In his greeting and prayers for the Thessalonians, Paul shifts the focus from the release *from* the trouble to positive things that can be produced and experienced *in* the time of trouble. What are they (1:4–5, 11–12; 2:16–17; 3:5, 16,18)?

BEFORE THE END

Paul shows that the end had not yet come. What had still to take place (2:1–12)?

IDLENESS

Paul commands those who were idle to 'settle down and earn the bread they eat' (3:12; cf. 1 Thess 5:14). On what authority does he make this command (3:6,12)? With what example does he back it up (3:7–10)? With what action is the church to enforce this (3:6,14–15)? Why do you think he regarded this issue as so important?

How would you apply the principle behind these instructions today when, because of economic conditions, unemployment is very high?

UNIT 4

Paul's Care for the Churches

CORINTH AND PAUL'S RELATIONSHIP WITH THE CORINTHIANS

Corinth was the city where Paul almost gave up. After all that he had been through in the course of his second missionary journey (Acts 15:39–18:32) we might think that he could face anything. But Corinth, one of the largest and most important centres of trade and industry in the Mediterranean, was daunting.

The skyline was dominated by a rocky mound on top of which sat the temple of Aphrodite, the Greek goddess of love, just one of a number of pagan temples in the city. These functioned as places to meet and eat, and many of the city's food shops got their meat supplies from them. There was one modest synagogue, and a Jewish community formed part of the very mixed cos-

mopolitan population of about 250,000 freemen and perhaps double that number of slaves.

The city may or may not have deserved the reputation for immorality that citizens of its rival, Athens, had encouraged in ancient times. But some impression of the sort of people whom Paul encountered there may be gained from his description of what some Corinthian Christians had previously been (1 Cor 6:9–11). He had been scared (1 Cor 2:3), but God had reassured him in a vision that, however unlikely it might have seemed, many of these people were his (Acts 18:9–10). Encouraged by this, Paul made Corinth his base for the next eighteen months (AD 50–51). At the end of that time he left

Looking across the ruins of Corinth to the Acrocorinth. In the foreground is the start of the Lechaion road which leads off to the right to the ancient harbour some four miles (6.5 km) away.

behind a Christian group as varied in its ethnic, socio-economic and religious origins as was the city in which it existed.

1 and 2 Corinthians testify to Paul's continuing relationship with this young church. News travelled back and forth by means of messengers and delegates both from the church and from the apostle (e.g. 1 Cor 1:11; 16:17; 2 Cor 7:13–15),

and there was at least one other visit by Paul to Corinth (2 Cor 2:1; 12:14; 13:1).

These letters, therefore, are fruits of a living – and lively – relationship. There were certainly more than two letters from Paul to the church at Corinth, and when we look at 2 Corinthians we shall discuss the possible sequence of contacts and correspondence. First, however, we shall give our attention to 1 Corinthians.

---

1 CORINTHIANS

'you are the body of Christ'

BACKGROUND BRIEFING

This letter was written from Ephesus, in Asia (1 Cor 16:8), towards the end of the three years which Paul spent there on his third missionary expedition (c. AD55).

> ### TO THINK ABOUT . . .
> 1 Corinthians is the longest letter we have looked at so far, but it is still important to read it through at a sitting. As you do so, make brief notes on what you discover about the Corinthian church – both good and bad! – and any specific issue to which this letter was a response.

THE CHURCH AT CORINTH

1 Corinthians portrays a church rich in spiritual experience, especially in the more spectacular manifestations of the Spirit, but deeply divided and suffering from pride and lack of mutual consideration. There were not only various

Christian 'parties', but also divisions between rich and poor. Many in the church had been converted from paganism, and though there was wonderful evidence of how God had transformed them, some problems of behaviour and attitude remained. The church had been founded by Paul and to a large extent continued to follow his teaching, but there was confusion on some important matters.

WHAT PROMPTED PAUL TO WRITE?

Paul had received reports of the church at Corinth which spoke of division (1:11; 11:18) and immorality (5:1). There had also been a letter to Paul from the church, asking various questions relating to marriage and 'food offered to idols' (7:1; 8:1). The apostle was hoping to visit them himself, and he wanted to prepare the way for the visit, including forewarning them to be ready with 'the collection for God's people' (16:1–7).

The remains of the Greek Temple of Apollo at Corinth. It is one of the oldest temples in Greece, dating from about the middle of the sixth-century BC, and so was old when Paul saw it.

A JOURNEY THROUGH 1 CORINTHIANS

> **TO THINK ABOUT . . .**
>
> Before sorting out the wide-ranging main content of this letter, look through it and note its structure, following the standard letter pattern found on page 39.

OPENING SECTION

a. Address (1:1–2)

There was a Sosthenes (*v.*1) who was ruler of the synagogue at Corinth when Paul preached there (Acts 18:17). This was probably the same man, now a Christian and working with Paul. Paul typically uses the very first opportunity to press home his major concerns, which in this instance are holiness and unity (*v.*2).

b. Greeting (1:3)

c. Thanksgiving (1:4–9)

Paul's thanksgiving for these Christians is directed to God for his gift and work, and from that perspective the thanksgiving for the past and present leads into confidence for the future.

MAIN CONTENT (1:10–16:12)

CLOSING SECTION

a. Personal news (16:13–18)

The personal section which by convention concluded ancient Greek letters was frequently utilised by Paul to convey some deeply felt exhortation to his readers, as he does here (*vv.*13–14).

b. Greetings and farewell (16:19–24)

Aquila and Priscilla (or Prisca) (v.19) had opened their home to Paul in Corinth (Acts 18:1–4), and now the home of this remarkable couple was the base for the church being established in Ephesus.

Paul's last sentence reinforces his plea for unity – instead of sending his own greetings to the Corinthians, he tells them to 'Greet one another . . .' (v.20). Not a phrase is wasted!

WHAT THE LETTER WAS ABOUT

This long letter, rather than following one argument or theme throughout, deals with several different matters in turn. The first step towards understanding the content is therefore to break it down into sections according to the subjects discussed.

TO THINK ABOUT . . .
Read through 1:10–16:12, identifying the main subject divisions.

The material could be considered in the following blocks, though the larger sections could obviously be subdivided into smaller units:

1:10–4:21	a problem in the church– divisions;
5:1–13	a problem in the church – a case of incest;
6:1–8	a problem in the church – taking fellow believers to court;
6:9–20	a problem in the church – sexual immorality;
7:1–40	questions about marriage and remaining unmarried;
8:1–11:1	questions about food that has been sacrificed to idols;
11:2–14:40	issues arising from the church's worship;
15:1–58	misunderstandings about the resurrection;
16:1–4	the collection for God's people at Jerusalem;
16:5–8	a visit from Paul;
16:9–11	a visit from Timothy;
16:12	a visit from Apollos.

We can see how Paul begins by tackling certain problems in the church that have come to his notice, then he replies to particular questions that the church itself had put to him, going on to deal with various matters pertaining to worship and their understanding of the resurrection (again referring constantly to specific issues for that church at that time), concluding with some practical arrangements.

WHAT IT MEANS FOR US

Just glancing through the outline demonstrates how much this letter is a response to a specific situation. Paul wrote to particular people whom he knew well about matters which involved and concerned them in the city of Corinth in AD 55.

So what meaning can it possibly have for us, in our very different circumstances? The fact that it forms part of the New Testament demonstrates that the church recognised that there was value in this letter for Christians beyond the particular time and place of its original purpose. It remains, however, a real letter to real people, and we should not read it as if it were written directly to us, addressing our problems in the context of our present circumstances.

We shall derive more benefit by first asking what exactly did it say to *them* in their situation, and why, and then considering what Paul would say if he were writing to *us* today. What would concern him about our life and faith? What answers would he give to our questions?

Once we have discovered what the letter said to them, the task is to distinguish between what is true and valid for all time everywhere, and therefore applies directly to us as well, and what was tied to their specific situation and which therefore cannot be applied directly to our circumstances. Our situation, though not identical, may appear similar in some respects, so that a similar application may be drawn, but we must take great care to understand as much as we can of the situation originally addressed so that we can see if our own question relates to the same sort of issue.

Whatever instruction is given in the letter will be based upon certain underlying principles: if we can discern what these are, we may be able to apply them to other problems including ours. This process demands great care and honesty. In addition to understanding the original readers and their background, we must also know ourselves. We have to sift out which of our own attitudes and opinions are derived from these eternally valid principles, and which have grown out of our own culture and social, educational or religious background.

A CASE STUDY –
WOMEN PARTICIPATING IN WORSHIP

The instruction Paul gives the Corinthians on this theme (see 11:2–16 and 14:33–36) demands the kind of careful approach we have described. We shall examine it in three steps by asking:

● what is the context in which this instruction is given?
● what exactly is the instruction?
● with what arguments does Paul support it?

Having done that, we will be better able to discuss how this teaching applies to us.

THE CONTEXT

Both these passages fall within the section dealing with public worship (11:2–14:40).

> **TO THINK ABOUT . . .**
> Read through the whole section, looking for Paul's overriding concerns about what should characterise the church's worship.

Paul wants the church to be built up and strengthened, and that is the criterion by which he wants his readers to evaluate their actions and practices. These should spring from genuine love, shown in consideration for one another. Vocal participation in their gatherings for worship is encouraged, but always in order to benefit others; they should equally be prepared to remain silent or to give way to another so that maximum benefit might come to all. The result will be vital, orderly worship, which not only builds up the church but also makes a positive impression on any outsiders who come in.

The specific issues encountered in this section need to be set within this context. The underlying concern in each instance is: 'What sort of worship will build up the church in love, manifest consideration for others and not put unnecessary obstacles in the way of non-Christians meeting God among them?'

THE INSTRUCTION

> **TO THINK ABOUT . . .**
> Look at the two passages in question and state as briefly as possible what exactly Paul tells the Corinthian women to do.

If the exercise above seems too simple a task, be assured that much confusion amongst Christians over the interpretation of various passages would be avoided if they carefully ensured that what they argue about is what the passage actually says. In our two passages, the instructions Paul gives to women are:

○ Wear a head-covering when you pray or prophesy.
○ Do not speak in the church.

Perhaps this task is not as simple as it first appeared. The two instructions seem at first sight to cancel each other out. Since there can be no doubt from 11:2–16 that Paul expected women to be praying and prophesying, activities which involve speech, he cannot mean by the second instruction that women are not to speak at all. We must therefore go back to the passage and ask, 'What *sort* of speaking is prohibited?'

TO THINK ABOUT . . .

Read the passage in its immediate context (14:26–40). What clues can you find as to what exactly Paul wanted to stop from:

■ the main concern of the section in which the instruction comes (14:26–40);
■ how the point is developed (*vv.34–35*)?

It is disorder in public worship which Paul is concerned about (*vv.33,40*), so the sort of speaking that he forbids must be disruptive of orderly worship. The alternative to this speaking is to 'be in submission' and 'ask their own husbands at home'. This suggests that the instruction relates not to the contributions which women were making in public worship (something which, far from forbidding, Paul simply asks them to do in a fitting manner (11:2–16)), but to an unruly commenting or clamouring for explanations, perhaps of prophecies.

THE ARGUMENTS

We move now from the 'what' question to the 'why', a crucial one when we come to evaluate the way in which Paul's teaching applies to us. We have already had to dig beneath the surface of the instruction in 14:33–35 to discover what was meant. We shall now turn to the more complex passage in 11:2–16 where the conclusion that women should wear a head covering when they pray or prophesy in public worship is supported by various arguments.

TO THINK ABOUT . . .

Look in this passage for six arguments by which Paul supports his conclusion.

Paul argues from:

a. Headship (3–5)

○ There is an order of headship: God–Christ–man–woman.
○ A women should express her respect for her head in this order by wearing a head covering when she prays or prophesies.

b. Disgrace (5–6)

○ It is disgraceful for a woman to have her hair cut.
○ To have her head uncovered has the same effect as having her hair cut.
○ It is therefore disgraceful for a woman to have her head uncovered.

c. Creation (7–10)

○ Woman was created from man and for man.
○ She should therefore show that she is under authority by wearing a head covering.

d. The angels (10)

○ He doesn't explain it, just states it!

e. The nature of things (13–15)

○ It seems proper for a woman to have long hair, but not for a man.
○ This long hair is intended as a covering for her head.

f. The practice of the churches (16)

○ This is the custom of Paul and all the churches.

BRIDGING THE CULTURE GAP

The key question in interpreting this for our own day is how much is specific to the culture into which Paul spoke and what elements are universally and eternally valid?

Three of these arguments (*b, e, f*) refer to social custom and ideas of decency. We could therefore reason that in cultures where it is not considered disgraceful for a woman to cut her hair or appear in public with her head uncovered, the specific application of these verses does not apply. There is, however, an underlying principle, that of not offending the prevailing sense of decency. That principle may very well be applied in any culture, in ways appropriate to that culture.

The argument about the angels (*d.*) is obscure, and it is therefore hazardous for us to build a case upon it; we should always interpret the obscure in Scripture in the light of what is clear. The early church certainly believed that angels were present when they were at worship, and this would provide a further incentive to reverence.

We are left then with two theological arguments, from an order of headship (*a.*) and from creation (*c.*). The second of these Paul immediately answers himself (*vv.*11–12), showing that in fact man derives from woman as much as woman derives from man. And anyway 'in the Lord' there is not dominance of one over the other but a mutuality. He is struggling with the tension between the norms of a society, in his case built on Judaism (*v.*7), and the radical transformation in relationships effected by being 'in the Lord' (*v.*11). Again, we can learn from how Paul deals with this tension, desiring both to live out the implications of life in Christ and to avoid unnecessarily scandalising society or leaving the Christians themselves vulnerable to temptation.

The most substantial argument is the first, where Paul seems to begin from a fundamental principle of an order of headship. Once more we have to ensure that we see exactly what is said. The word 'head' is used in two ways in these verses, meaning either the part of the body or conveying the idea of authority, depending on the context. In Greek the words for 'man' and 'woman' are the same as those for 'husband' and 'wife', so we have to decide whether Paul is speaking about men and women in general or specifically about wives and husbands.

There are of course various interpretations, but we can turn to other passages which might throw some light on Paul's teaching here. In Ephesians 5:21–33 and Colossians 3:18–19 Paul speaks of husbands and wives in the context of Christ's headship. We see there twin qualities; firstly, self-denying love on the part of someone exercising responsibility for another, and, secondly, submission on the part of someone acknowledging authority in another. Both these qualities are

A hair-style worn by Roman ladies. The hair was arranged in three rows of curls over the forehead. A long plait was wound round the back of the head.

modelled by Christ himself, and they are to be manifested in marriage by husband and wife respectively as an expression of their reverence for Christ.

Reading our passage in the light of that concern, we see the principle: even as she participates in public worship, making her own contribution as part of the body of Christ, a woman should show respect for her husband. In that society a woman appearing in public with her head uncovered would either be flaunting her refusal to be under her husband's authority or would be considered immoral. Either way her 'head', i.e. her husband, is dishonoured in the eyes of those who see her. This was apparently going on in the Corinthian church (could it have been a particularly sore point with husbands whose wives had become Christians while they had not?). As he does with regard to other issues, Paul wants them to accept restraint on what they could argue was their new freedom in Christ in order to avoid causing any to stumble, either in the church or outside it (cf. 10:31–33).

MAKING THE APPLICATION TO OURSELVES

> ### TO THINK ABOUT . . .
>
> From the teaching about the participation of women in worship found in 11:2–14:40, what do you think were:
>
> - the principles on which Paul's teaching was based;
> - the specific applications of those principles in the Corinthian setting?
>
> How might these principles be applied in your own church's worship?

The use of a timeless principle to support a particular application does not mean that the application itself becomes timeless. In the situation in Corinth, a principle was certainly at stake – that, even in her new standing in Christ, a woman should show respect for her husband. But the application of that principle – that women should cover their heads when participating in public worship – was in terms which were culturally appropriate in that society. If we intend to apply it to ourselves, we have to find a way of putting the principle into practice which is culturally appropriate in our own society.

EXPLORING FURTHER

There is far more in 1 Corinthians than the issue we have been discussing, but it has served as a case study providing an example of an approach which can readily be applied to other strands of teaching. Tongues and Prophecy is one other from the same section on worship.

TONGUES AND PROPHECY

Examine Paul's teaching on the use of tongues and prophecy in public worship.

a. The context

Read through the whole section (11:2–14:40) identifying the main concerns which Paul displays about the church's worship and any general principles from which he works.

b. The instruction

What exactly does Paul tell them to do in connection with the use of tongues and prophecy?

c. The reasoning

With what arguments does Paul support the guidelines which he gives?

d. Applying it to ourselves

From the teaching you have examined, list *a.* principles and *b.* specific applications of these principles to the Corinthian church.

Are the same applications relevant to your own church, or could the same principles be applied practically in other ways?

2 CORINTHIANS

'through God's mercy we have this ministry'

BACKGROUND BRIEFING

SEQUENCE OF EVENTS

In both 1 and 2 Corinthians there are a number of references to letters and visits (e.g. 1 Cor 4:18–21; 5:9; 16:5–9; 2 Cor 1:15–17; 2:1; 2:3–4,9; 7:8; 12:14; 13:1,10; 13:2). Taking these with the account of Paul's movements in Acts 18:1–20:3, we can attempt to piece together the sequence of events surrounding Paul's relationship with the Corinthian church. The two letters we have may be placed within that sequence of events. It was probably something like this:

a. Paul in Corinth (Acts 18:1–17)

This is Paul's **first visit** to the city, during which the church is founded.

b. Paul based in Ephesus (Acts 18:18–19:41)

○ He writes a **letter** including the instruction 'not to associate with sexually immoral people' (1 Cor 5:9).
○ He receives news of divisions and other problems in the church (1 Cor 1:11) and also a letter from them with various questions (1 Cor 7:1).
○ He writes a **letter** dealing with these problems and questions (1 Cor).
○ He makes a **second visit** to Corinth which turns out to be painful, both for the church and for the apostle (2 Cor 2:1–2; a second visit is also implied in 2 Cor 12:14; 13:1).
○ He writes a severe **letter** 'out of great distress and anguish of heart and with many tears' (2 Cor 2:3–4,9; 7:8).

The Street of the Curetes in Ephesus. The street was a ceremonial way and was lined with sculptures and public buildings. From Ephesus Paul kept up his contacts with the church at Corinth.

c. Paul journeys through Macedonia (Acts 20:1–2)

○ Anxious for news of the Corinthians, Paul breaks off his ministry in Troas and seeks out Titus, who had been in Corinth, probably delivering the stern letter (2 Cor 2:12–13). When they meet, the news is very good, of 'godly sorrow' that had produced repentance, and of a renewed warmth of affection for Paul (2 Cor 7:5–16).

○ Paul writes another **letter**, in response to what he has heard (2 Cor).

d. Paul back in Corinth (Acts 20:2–3)

The promised **third visit** (2 Cor 12:14; 13:1) takes place when Paul's journey through Macedonia takes him to Greece. It was very probably Corinth where Paul stayed three months (Acts 20:3).

2 CORINTHIANS – ONE LETTER OR SEVERAL?

The sequence outlined above includes three visits and four letters from Paul to the Corinthians. So which of these letters are 1 and 2 Corinthians? The straightforward solution is to identify 1 Corinthians with the second of these four letters, and 2 Corinthians with the fourth. On reading through 2 Corinthians, however, many have noted abrupt changes in subject or tone at various points, leading to the suggestion that our 2 Corinthians is in fact not one letter but a collection of letters or parts of letters. It would have been an acceptable practice to make such a collection and to join various writings together in one scroll of convenient length. It has to be said, however, that 2 Corinthians appears in its present form even in the earliest existing manuscripts.

The most marked change in mood occurs at 9:15–10:1 with a sudden switch from an atmosphere of glad encouragement to a forceful assertion of apostolic authority and stern warning to those in Corinth who had been trying to discredit Paul. This continues until the end of the letter. Other 'seams' in the letter have been observed at 2:13/14, shifting from the account of Paul's movements to a defence of his apostleship, and the same shift in reverse at 7:4/5. Could 2:14–7:4 therefore be an insertion? Within that block itself there seems to be a break in the thought at 6:13 which is resumed at 7:2. This is just one example of the thinking which has been applied to this letter.

The possibility that 2 Corinthians contains parts of various letters invites us to look within it for the 'missing' letters from our sequence. Some have thought that 2 Corinthians 6:14–7:1 could be part of that earliest letter 'not to associate with sexually immoral prople' (1 Cor 5:9). Still more support has been found for the suggestion that we have the third 'severe' letter preserved in 2 Corinthians 10–13, or that this is perhaps a separate fifth letter written when Paul's apostleship again came under attack at a later date.

On the other hand, a change in tone or subject does not necessarily imply a different letter. A writer can digress, follow through a thought and then return to the theme, as indeed Paul does in other letters. A profoundly personal letter written with much emotion is also less likely to keep to a strictly logical structure. Factors such as the arrival of more news could effect a change in tone, especially in a letter written or dictated over a period of days.

The 'insertions' may not be so incongruous as is claimed. 2 Corinthians 6:14–7:1, for example, makes very good sense where it is, if it is taken to refer not to the sexually immoral but to the false teachers who were stirring up trouble in Corinth. Scholars who want to argue for partitioning up the letter also have to explain, among other things, why the various sections were inserted where they were.

PAUL'S MINISTRY

Whatever conclusion is reached as to the unity or otherwise of the letter, we undoubtedly have in 2 Corinthians a document which comes from the apostle's heart. The immediacy and urgency of his love and concern for this troubled and volatile Christian community comes through. One of the great values of this letter is the insight it gives into Paul's own ministry. He speaks of its source, its motivation, its goal, its cost and, albeit reluctantly, his qualifications for it.

A JOURNEY THROUGH 2 CORINTHIANS

OPENING SECTION

a. Address (1:1)

b. Greeting (1:2)

c. Thanksgiving (1:3–11)

Both Paul and the Corinthian Christians had to endure suffering, but Paul finds cause for thanksgiving and praise in the comfort they received from God in their trouble, in an experience of deliverance, and in their confidence in God.

MAIN CONTENT (1:12–13:10)

a. Paul's defence (1:12–7:16)

○ A clear conscience (1:12–14).
○ Explanation for the deferring of his visit (1:15–2:2).
○ Explanation for Paul's 'stern letter' (2:3–11).
○ A God-given ministry and competence (2:12–3:6).
○ A glorious ministry of the Spirit that brings righteousness (3:7–18).
○ Treasure in jars of clay (4:1–18).
○ 'At home' and 'away' (5:1–10).
○ The ministry of reconciliation (5:11–6:2).

○ Servants of God proved through sufferings (6:3–13).
○ Appeal to separate from false teachers (6:14–7:1).
○ Joy upon hearing of the Corinthian Christians and their response to Paul's letter (7:2–16).

b. The grace of giving (8:1–9:15)

c. Further defence (10:1–12:13)

○ Warning that Paul will come with severity if need be (10:1–6).
○ Criticisms and slurs on Paul (10:7–18).
○ Paul and the 'super-apostles' (11:1–15).
○ Paul boasts about his sufferings (11:16–33).
○ Paul boasts about his spiritual experience (12:1–6).
○ Paul's 'thorn in the flesh' and God's grace (12:7–10).
○ Why he has had to 'boast' (12:11–13).

d. Preparation for Paul's next visit (12:14–13:10)

CLOSING SECTION

Farewell; final exhortation and greetings (13:11–14)

Examples of Roman pottery and 'jars of clay' from the first century.

Reproduced by courtesy of the Trustees of the British Museum

EXPLORING FURTHER

SORROW AND JOY

What was there about the Christian community in Corinth which *a.* grieved Paul, and *b.* gave him joy? (Referring also to 1 Corinthians will clearly help.)

'TREASURE IN JARS OF CLAY'

Explore what can be learned about Paul's own ministry from 2 Corinthians, making notes under the following headings:

a. terms used for those exercising such a ministry (e.g. 'God's fellow-workers');

b. source of his ministry;

c. goals;

d. motivation;

e. resources available to him;

f. content of his preaching;

g. methods;

h. personal cost of exercising this ministry;

i. rewards;

j. qualifications.

How far should this be a pattern for ministry today?

Paul's Gospel

Galatians and Romans are the two letters in which Paul sets out most clearly the gospel which he preached. Many of the themes and arguments of one therefore appear also in the other, and to that extent they are similar. In style and manner, however, they could hardly be less alike. One was an intensely personal letter to churches which Paul himself had founded and

pastored; the other went to a church which Paul had not even visited. One has the urgency of a reaction to a crisis; the other the calm, measured style of a systematic presentation of doctrine free of the pressure of some immediate threat. It has been said that Galatians is the rough sketch and Romans the polished sculpture.

GALATIANS

'Christ has set us free'

BACKGROUND BRIEFING

GENTILE CHRISTIANS AND JUDAISM

The news from Galatia greatly disturbed Paul. On the first missionary journey he and Barnabas (Acts 13–14) had experienced many hardships and times of danger. They had returned to Antioch, however, thrilled with what God had done, leaving behind a string of young churches (e.g. Derbe, Lystra, Iconium) in what is now central and southern Turkey. The great news was that God had 'opened the door of faith to the Gentiles' (Acts 14:27).

Soon, however, disturbing reports reached Paul. Certain visitors followed in the footsteps of the apostles. Their purpose was not to encourage the young Christians in their new-found faith, but, as they saw it, to put them right. They claimed

to be followers of Christ, but in their view Paul's message to the Gentiles was unsatisfactory. They therefore wanted to discredit Paul in the eyes of these converts, and insist that they should comply with requirements 'essential' for any non-Jews who wished to become Christians.

As soon as he heard this, Paul responded with his letter to the Galatians. The problem, however, was not confined to this one occurrence. The place of Gentiles in what had begun as a movement within Judaism caused confusion and dispute elsewhere, even in Antioch and amongst the apostles themselves. Paul and Barnabas were therefore sent to Jerusalem, where a council of the apostles and elders considered the question (see 'A nettle that had to be grasped', page 32). Their conclusion was in harmony with Paul's letter to the churches in Galatia.

A scene in the vicinity of Derbe. In Paul's day this was the region of southern Galatia.

THE LETTER'S DATE

This suggests that the letter was written from Antioch before the Jerusalem Council (i.e. AD 48 or 49), making it the earliest letter of Paul that we have. An alternative view is that it was written up to three years after the Council, and that Paul refers to the visit to Jerusalem in Galatians 2:1–10. The details do not fit very naturally, however, and it is more likely that Paul referred there to an earlier visit (Acts 9:26–30 or 11:30). The relationship between these passages in Galatians and Acts is important for working out the chronology of Paul's life and mission and has a bearing on other issues, such as Paul's relationship with the Jerusalem church leaders. For the purpose of discovering the message of this letter, however, the exact date is not as important as the sort of problem which it was addressing. This, happily, is not difficult to uncover.

As with the letters to the Thessalonians, we shall first take an overview of the letter and then try to grasp its message.

INITIAL SURVEY

> **TO THINK ABOUT . . .**
> Read through the letter fairly quickly, making brief notes on:
>
> - the people to whom it was written;
> - Paul's attitude towards them;
> - any specific reasons for writing.

You may have noted the following points.

a. The letter's recipients

- They belonged to various churches in Galatia (1:2).
- The gospel of Jesus Christ was preached clearly to them, and they received the Holy Spirit and experienced miracles (3:1–5).
- Now, however, they seemed to be turning away from the Spirit to human effort (3:3).

○ Before becoming Christians they were caught up in ineffective forms of religion – to which they were now in danger of returning (4:8–10).

○ Paul himself preached the gospel to them and they had received him very warmly. Now their attitude to him seemed to have changed (4:12–16).

○ Some were persuaded to be circumcised (1:2–3).

b. Paul's attitude towards them

○ Paul has been astonished and perplexed by these Christians (1:6; 4:20).

○ There is sharp disappointment and dismay in Paul's tone (1:6; 3:1–5).

○ He is afraid lest all that was done amongst them should turn out to be for nothing (3:4; 4:11).

○ He loves them as dear children, and is in anguish for them (4:19).

○ He is very angry about those who brought other teaching into the churches (1:7–9; 4:17; 5:7–10,12; 6:12–13).

c. Specific reasons for writing

○ Some people came among the Christians propounding 'another gospel' (1:6–9; 5:10), so Paul wants to reaffirm the gospel which he preached to them (1:11–12).

○ Paul's motives were criticised, with the suggestion that he only preached as he did to please his hearers (1:10). He wants to defend his apostleship and the authority of the gospel he proclaimed (1:11–2:10).

○ The fellowship was troubled with internal conflict and pride (5:15,26).

A JOURNEY THROUGH GALATIANS

TO THINK ABOUT . . .
Referring to the standard letter pattern (page 39), look through the letter to the Galatians and note its structure.

---

any such sentiment, giving even greater force to the strong words which come where the thanksgiving might have been expected (1:6).

MAIN CONTENT (1:6–6:10)

The main body of the letter is taken up with the two concerns which have already surfaced in the address. After stating the problem (1:6–10), Paul first gives a defence of his own apostleship (1:11–2:21) and then sets about dealing with the 'other gospel' (3:1–6:10).

OPENING SECTION

a. Address (1:1–2)

Paul takes the first opportunity to assert the source of his authority as an apostle.

b. Greeting (1:3–5)

Even the greeting is used to emphasise the saving work of Christ and to root this in the will of God the Father.

c. Thanksgiving

Where is it?! Readers or listeners expecting a conventional word of thanks to God for them would have been startled by the total absence of

CLOSING SECTION

a. Personal news and greetings (6:11–17)

There is no personal news, but Paul takes up the pen to add a final greeting. Again, however, his main concerns take over and the signature grows into a further condemnation of those who had troubled them, and a reaffirmation of the gospel.

b. Farewell (6:18)

Despite all, they are still 'brothers'!

THE MESSAGE OF GALATIANS

We now look more closely at the main content of the letter.

a. Paul's apostleship (1:11–2:21)

> *TO THINK ABOUT . . .*
>
> **What evidence does Paul give in this section to support his claim that he was 'an apostle, sent not from men nor by man, but by Jesus Christ and God the Father . . .' (1:1)?**
>
> **Paul concludes that 'a man is not justified by observing the law, but by faith in Jesus Christ'. How did his own experience bear this out (see e.g. Phil 3:2–11)?**

b. The Good News (3:1–6:10)

Paul argues for the 'gospel of Christ', which he had preached to the Galatians, over against the 'other gospel' which was being presented to them. The two are contrasted in three areas, as set out below.

> *TO THINK ABOUT . . .*
>
> **Read each of these sections through and note the main point which is being made. Summarise briefly the argument of the section. It may prove helpful to read paragraph by paragraph, writing down in one sentence what each paragraph contributes to the argument.**

○ (3:1–25) **How the Christian is put right with God**
– observing the   Law   or believing the promise?

○ (3:26–5:15) **The Christian's status**
– slavery or sonship?

The 'basic principles' (4:3,8–10) refer to forces which held people in bondage through fear and produced a religion of obligation instead of gift. This is what the Galatians had known in paganism; Paul warns them against succumbing to the same sort of bondage through Judaizing Christianity.

○ (5:16–6:10) **The Christian's life-force**
– the sinful nature or the Spirit?

> *TO THINK ABOUT . . .*
>
> Taking all this together, what is the Good News?

ROMANS

'righteousness from God . . . through faith in Jesus Christ'

BACKGROUND BRIEFING

ROME AND ITS CHURCH

At first sight Romans seems to consist largely of a timeless exposition of Christian doctrine, more like a theological essay than a letter. And yet it was not published as a booklet on theology. It was a letter, sent to a particular group of people at a particular time. It is important to recognise this, not only because knowing Paul's purpose in writing will help us to understand the content and what it leads up to, but also because it will save us from the mistake of looking for all of Paul's theology in this one document. (It is an interesting exercise to go through Romans noting what important areas of Christian belief are *not* dealt with!)

Visitors from Rome, 'both Jews and converts to Judaism', were amongst the crowds in Jerusalem on the Day of Pentecost (Acts 2:10–11). Possibly some of them became the first Christians in Rome. In common with modern cities, first-century Rome both impressed and appalled visitors. Side by side with the magnificent buildings, aqueducts and streets, and the vibrancy of its multiracial population, were desperate social problems and evidence of crime and moral degradation.

The church would have been predominantly Gentile (see 1:5–6), but there were also Jews, while some of the Gentiles had embraced elements of Judaism. Though Paul had not yet visited the church, it is astonishing how many people he knew there (16:3–16). These included relatives, converts of Paul, and fellow workers such as his good friends Priscilla and Aquila, who had been with him in Corinth and Ephesus. This indicates something of the mobility of the Christian population, prompted in part by local persecutions.

The Roman Forum, looking from the Capitoline Hill and looking south-east. The Via Sacra, probably so called because it served various temples, runs from the lower left towards the famous Arch of Titus.

PAUL'S PURPOSE IN WRITING

Why did Paul write to this group of people at that particular time?

> *TO THINK ABOUT . . .*
>
> **What do 1:8–15 and 15:14–33 reveal about Paul's hopes and plans and Rome's place in them?**

Paul wanted to exercise a ministry in Rome, both in strengthening the church spiritually and in winning new converts. His vision, however, extended beyond Rome to the West. He hoped that the Roman church could provide financially for him to make a missionary journey to Spain (the word 'assist' in 15:24 can mean 'equip for an expedition'). First he had to go to Jerusalem to deliver the gift for the poor, but then he planned to journey to Rome.

If the church in Rome was to accept and support Paul in his mission, he would have to convince them not only of the desirability of such a mission but also of the trustworthiness of his preaching. His main purpose in writing as he did can be explained in these terms: he wanted to set out clearly the way of salvation as he proclaimed it, and to give a rationale for the mission to the Gentiles. It was also an opportunity to give a clear account of the apostolic gospel to a church which had not, to our knowledge, received teaching directly from an apostle (see 15:14–16).

From the content of the letter it can be inferred that there was some tension between Jew and Gentile in the Roman church, as indeed there was in most congregations. Paul urged them to accept one another, demonstrating that God accepted both on the same basis.

The letter was probably written from Corinth during Paul's third visit in AD57 (Gaius and Erastus, mentioned in 16:23, were inhabitants of Corinth).

A JOURNEY THROUGH ROMANS

Romans follows the standard letter pattern, with some variation.

OPENING SECTION

a. Address (1:1–7a)

Paul emphasises his calling as an apostle, and draws attention to important features of the gospel which he is called to proclaim:

○ it is testified to in the Scriptures;
○ it centres on Jesus Christ, descendant of David and Son of God, risen from the dead;
○ it is offered to the Gentiles.

b. Greeting (1:7b)

c. Thanksgiving (1:8–15)

Not knowing the church well, Paul's thanksgiving for them has to be in general terms, but it flows into an expression of his desire to be with them.

MAIN CONTENT (1:16–15:13)

CLOSING SECTION

a. Personal news and greetings (15:14–16:23)

Paul, speaking tactfully to a church over which he has not been exercising authority, points to his calling from God and its confirmation (15:14–22) and then tells them of his future plans, and his hope that they will assist him (15:23–32).

He finishes with a greeting (15:33), but then adds (16:1–2) a reference to Phoebe, a deacon from one of the Corinthian ports. It was probably Phoebe who carried the letter to Rome, and the list of personal greetings (16:3–23) would ensure her acceptance by the church.

b. Ascription of glory (16:25–27)

The letter concludes by giving glory to God for what has been expounded in the course of the letter. Just as in the opening address, the gospel is described as the proclamation of Jesus Christ, made known through the Scriptures and intended by God for all nations. This, says Paul, is 'my gospel'. He rests his case!

THE JOURNEY'S DETAILED ROUTE

THE TEACHING CONTENT

In addition to the letter pattern, another standard literary form is helpful for throwing light on the main content of Romans. Greek teachers often set out their discourses in the form of the diatribe. The teacher spoke as if he was in conversation with an audience, who put forward objections and raised questions. The argument was set out in the following elements:

○ statement of the idea being proposed (the thesis);
○ logical necessity for the thesis shown;
○ another statement of the thesis;
○ thesis demonstrated by an example;
○ thesis expounded;
○ objections to the thesis answered.

The main content of Romans is often described as falling into a theological section (ch 1–11) and a practical section (ch 12–15). When we apply the diatribe pattern to 1:16–11:36, the structure illuminates the way in which Paul's argument is developed. We shall therefore follow this Hellenistic teaching structure as we read the letter. The form, but not the content, owes much to Greek philosphy.

Paul trained as a rabbi, and his argument is supported throughout by a string of Old Testament texts, from which points are drawn out in the rabbinic manner. Indeed, one of his main contentions is that the gospel he preached was revealed in the Old Testament scriptures (1:2; 16:26). The letter could helpfully be understood as a sermon on Habakkuk 2:4, announced as the text in 1:17.

THE THEOLOGICAL ARGUMENT (1:16–11:36)

a. The thesis proposed (1:16–17)

Every phrase in this opening statement is important. It sets out the position to be demonstrated and defended, consisting of the following components:

○ the gospel is power for salvation;
○ it is for Jew and Gentile;
○ in it a righteousness is revealed which is from God;
○ this righteousness depends entirely on faith.

b. The logical necessity for what is proposed (1:18–3:20)

> *TO THINK ABOUT . . .*
> Read through this section paragraph by paragraph. Note how each part contributes to the development of the argument, leading to the conclusion in 3:9–20.

c. The thesis re-stated (3:21–31)

> *TO THINK ABOUT . . .*
> What amplification and explanation is given here of the terse opening statement (1:16–17)?

d. An example to demonstrate the truth of what is proposed (4:1–25)

In choosing Abraham as an example, Paul tackled the opponents of his position at what they regarded as one of their strongest points. Jewish teachers used Abraham as a prime example of someone justified by his works. Paul argues that Abraham demonstrates exactly the opposite, namely, that righteousness comes from God and is received by faith.

> *TO THINK ABOUT . . .*
> List the points Paul makes about:
>
> - how righteousness came to be credited to Abraham;
> - who are the 'offspring' of Abraham.

e. The thesis expounded (5:1–21)

The theme is developed in terms of the benefits to us of this justification and the way in which these have been achieved through Christ's work.

> *TO THINK ABOUT . . .*
> In *vv.*1–11, what is the new standing before God which those who have been justified by faith enjoy? What are its implications? How has this been accomplished for us?
>
> What contrasts does Paul draw between Adam and Christ in *vv.*12–21?

f. Objections answered (6:1–11:32)

Paul realises that his insistence that salvation comes not by keeping the Law but through what Christ has done will provoke questions and objections. He deals with a number of these in this next section, sometimes posing a question in order to answer it, at other times dealing with an implied objection. An idea or word in the closing sentences of one section often provides a springboard into the next.

○ **Gift and Obligation (6:1–23)**

– 'dead to sin . . . alive to God in Christ Jesus'

> *TO THINK ABOUT . . .*
> Summarise in a sentence or two Paul's answers to the following questions:
>
> - 'Shall we go on sinning, so that grace may increase?' (6:1–14);
> - 'Shall we sin because we are not under law but under grace? (6:15–23).

○ **Law and Spirit (7:1–8:39)**

– 'released from the law . . . serve in the new way of the Spirit'

- The argument stated (7:1–6)

Having shown that by dying with Christ the Christian is set free from the hold of sin, Paul now argues that in Christ the Christian has also died to the law. He makes the point by means of an analogy with a marriage bond: once broken by the death of one partner, the other is free to marry again. There has been a death which has broken our obligation to the law, and we are therefore free to belong to another, namely God. We serve him not by the law but by the Spirit.

Paul uses the word 'law' in different ways, sometimes within the same verse. It sometimes refers to the Old Testament Mosaic Law, which he also calls 'the written code' (7:6), but elsewhere it means simply a principle or force as we might talk of 'the law of gravity'. In 7:21,23, for example, the idea is that sin, like gravity, exerts a downward pull so that whenever you want to do good you find yourself battling against a force pulling you in the opposite direction. Usually the context makes it quite clear which sense is intended. When he speaks of 'God's law' (7:22,25), he could mean either the Mosaic Law or, more broadly, that which is right in God's sight.

- Questions about the law (7:7–25)

Paul immediately has to counter objections that his argument denigrates the law (7:7–25).

TO THINK ABOUT . . .

What are the main points which Paul makes in answer to the questions:

- **Does this mean that the law itself is sin? (7:7–12)**
- **How then can something good produce death? (7:13–25)**

- Life in the Spirit (8:1–39)

    A new 'law' (8:1–17)

    The objections answered, Paul is free to pick up again the train of thought from 7:6. He shows that, far from undermining the law, it is only by what God has done in Christ and by the Spirit within us that 'the righteous requirements of the law might be fully met in us' (8:4). The obedience which is incumbent upon the Christian is not the slavery of the law, but the obligation of children and heirs (8:1–17).

TO THINK ABOUT . . .

What is the nature and the result of the work of the Spirit in those who belong to Christ?

    A glorious hope (8:18–39)

    It could be that some of Paul's readers, enduring trouble or persecution, would ask, 'If we are children of God, why are we suffering as we are? If God's Spirit gives life, why are we facing death?'

TO THINK ABOUT . . .

How is such bewilderment answered in this section?

In the broader context of the 'righteousness from God', on what grounds can a person have confidence that he or she cannot be condemned (see also 8:1ff)?

○ **God's Promise to Israel (9:1–11:32)**

There remains one terrible anomaly. The people of Israel, God's chosen ones, so richly privileged, had not entered into salvation. This caused Paul deep sorrow and perplexity. He would have been ready, if it were possible, even to lose his own salvation so that they might receive it. It is in this spirit, not of dispassionate theoretical discussion but of anguished searching for an answer to the question, 'Why are my own people not saved?', that he probes the deep mysteries of God's purpose in election.

The train of thought is clear if it is followed as a succession of questions. Read one section at a time, seeing how the particular question is answered.

- the anomaly stated (9:1–5);
- has God's promise to Abraham failed? (9:6–13);
- is God unjust, in choosing one and not the other? (9:14–18);
- so why does God blame people whose hearts are hardened to him? (9:19–29);
- why has Israel failed to obtain righteousness even though they pursued it, whereas the Gentiles obtained it when they had not pursued it? (9:30–10:21);
- did God, then, reject his people? (11:1–10);
- have they fallen beyond recovery? (11:11–24);

- the wonderful conclusion (11:25–32) – God's election of Israel has not failed; they are disobedient now so that the Gentiles may be brought in. When the Jews are saved, it will be on the same basis as the Gentiles – the mercy of God.

g. Conclusion (11:33–36)

The theological argument concludes appropriately with an outpouring of praise for the God out of whose wisdom and sheer self-giving has come this plan of salvation for Jew and Gentile alike.

Orthodox Jews gather for prayer and the reading of the Torah at the Western Wall in Jerusalem. Paul's 'heart's desire and prayer to God for the Israelites is that they may be saved.'

THE TEACHING APPLIED (12:1–15:13)

Paul's great exposition of the gospel has shown that we are saved by God's mercy. The response to this mercy is indicated in 12:1–2. It is to be in lives wholly given to God, bodies dedicated to his service and minds renewed so that life no longer takes its character from the world, but is in harmony with God's will.

This is worked out practically in three broad areas:

○ Living to please God in the church (12:3–21);
○ Living to please God in the world (13:1–14);
○ Glorifying God by coping with diversity (14:1–15:13).

TO THINK ABOUT . . .

How are the following themes from the theological argument applied practically in this section:

- mercy;
- life in Christ and the sinful nature;
- God's acceptance of all?

How does the conclusion of this section support Paul's desire for a mission to Spain (15:7–13)?

EXPLORING FURTHER

ROUGH SKETCH – FINISHED SCULPTURE

What themes, ideas and arguments from the letter to the Galatians are more fully expounded in the letter to the Romans? How do you explain the difference in tone?

LIFE IN THE SPIRIT

According to Romans, what is the role of the Holy Spirit in the 'Good News of righteousness from God'?

IMPACT

The letter to the Romans has profoundly affected the course of church – and world – history. This is illustrated through the impact that reading the letter had on such people as Augustine in the fourth century and Martin Luther in the sixteenth century. What impact has studying the letter had on you?

UNIT 6

Letters from Prison

MINISTRY CONTINUES IN PRISON

Paul did eventually reach Rome in AD 60, as a prisoner awaiting trial before the Emperor. It was two years before the case was heard, and during this period, though his movements were restricted, Paul was able to live in a rented house and receive visitors. We cannot be certain what happened when the trial took place, but it seems that Paul was aquitted and set free to continue his missionary work among the Gentiles (2 Timothy 4:16–17). It is probable that he embarked on a fourth and final missionary journey, not recorded in Acts, perhaps reaching Spain as he had planned and even revisiting Asia Minor. In AD 64, however, he was back in Rome, a prisoner again, but this time in the grimmer surroundings of the Mamertine prison. Here, during a vicious backlash of persecution in the reign of the Emperor Nero, he was executed.

Paul clearly endured imprisonments other than those of which we read in Acts (see 2 Corinthians 11:23). We know from Paul's letters that he endured severe suffering when he was in Asia Minor, whose capital city was Ephesus (e.g. 1 Cor 15:32; 2 Cor 1:8) and he may well have been imprisoned during that time (*c.* AD 55). It is not impossible that one or more of these 'prison letters' was written in Ephesus, but Paul's first imprisonment in Rome seems the most likely setting for the four letters which we shall consider in this unit.

In previous units we have dealt with only one or two New Testament writings. There are four in this unit and although we cannot examine them as thoroughly as we did, for example, the letter to the Romans, we shall read all four, aiming to grasp the main thrust of each and to acquire an awareness of its contents and purpose. You may find the following procedure helpful:

○ first read the background notes;
○ then read the letter fairly quickly, noting anything you discover about *a.* the recipients; *b.* the writer's attitude to them; *c.* any specific reasons for writing; *d.* the main issues dealt with and points made;
○ finally read the letter through more closely with the help of the outline.

PHILIPPIANS

'fellowship in the gospel'

BACKGROUND BRIEFING

Philippi was the first church which Paul founded in Europe (Acts 16:11–40), and it held a special place in his heart. The city had the status of a Roman colony, and its people were proud of their Roman citizenship. The first Christian converts there (Lydia, a prosperous businesswoman, and the town jailer, probably a retired soldier) were representative of the city's commercial success and strong military background.

It was one of the few places where Paul was unable to begin his proclamation of Christ in the synagogue, simply because there were not enough Jews in Philippi for a synagogue to be built. There is not a single quotation from the Old Testament in this letter to a thoroughly Gentile church.

Looking along the city walls of Philippi. Beyond the trees to the left of the field flows a small river. In this area it is likely, therefore, that Paul and his companions 'went to the river, where we expected to find a place of prayer' (Acts 16:13).

A JOURNEY THROUGH PHILIPPIANS

OPENING SECTION

a. Address (1:1)

Whereas predominantly Jewish Christian churches naturally patterned their structure on the synagogue, ruled by elders, the Gentile church in Philippi referred to its leaders as overseers, a term for a civic official.

b. Greeting (1:2)

c. Thanksgiving (1:3–11)

Paul's prayer of thanks for the Philippians spills over into intercession for them.

MAIN CONTENT (1:12–4:9)

The motif of example and imitation runs through the letter (e.g. 2:5; 3:17; 4:9). As well as the clear appeal to follow the example of Christ (2:5–11), the news Paul gives of himself and other leaders serves to illustrate lives patterned on Christ – and the mentions of the gospel's opponents indicate the opposite of such a life.

a. The example of Paul's attitude to his circumstances (1:12–30)

Good coming out of suffering (1:12–14) is going to be a recurrent theme in this letter.

'Selfish ambition', the motive of Paul's rivals (1:15–17), is the opposite of the attitude which this letter commends.

Although the Philippians no doubt prayed for Paul's release from prison (1:19), that was not necessarily what Paul meant when he talked about the deliverance which he was confident of receiving. For him, victory meant the exaltation of Christ, whether that was to be by his life or by his death (1:20). Indeed, if it were up to him, he would choose death, because he wanted to 'be with Christ' (1:24). His willingness to remain is for their sakes, not for his.

The encouragement to stand firm for the gospel (1:27–30) stems from the example of Paul himself.

b. The example of Christ's humility (2:1–18)

To be 'united with Christ' (2:1) is the essence of salvation. In *vv*.6–11 Paul seems to be quoting from a hymn sung by the early Christians. We do not possess a first-century Christian hymnbook, but this and other poetic fragments in the letters such as 1 Timothy 3:16 indicate that from an early date Christians expressed profound truths about Christ in the form of hymns.

The theme, Christ's self-emptying, humble obedience and death followed by his exaltation, is to be the pattern for those who follow him.

The Roman forum in Philippi, where probably Paul and Silas were brought before the local magistrates.

Paul himself takes the pattern of Christ in his willingness to be 'poured out like a drink offering' for them (17).

c. The example of two fellow servants (2:19–30)

Timothy was like Christ in being concerned for the interests of others (2:20), and Epaphroditus was ready to give his life (2:30).

d. The example of Paul's heavenward goal (3:1–4:9)

Opponents of the gospel again serve as counter-examples (3:1–4). Though he had more reason than any of his opponents for putting confidence in his human privileges and achievements, Paul wants to know Christ, gain Christ, be found in Christ, exercise faith in Christ, share in the death and resurrection of Christ (3:7–14). He lives looking heavenwards.

The Philippians are exhorted to look heavenwards, not like those whose 'mind is on earthly things' (3:17–4:1). To people conscious of the privileges of their Roman citizenship, the reminder that their 'citizenship was in heaven' would be telling (3:20).

This heavenward perspective exposes the pettiness of quarrels between people 'whose names are in the book of life' (4:2–4).

CLOSING SECTION

a. Personal news (4:10–20)

The warmth of friendship and the reality of the partnership between Paul and the church at Philippi is evident in these paragraphs.

b. Final Greetings and farewell (4:21–23)

Caesar's household (4:22) refers not to relatives of Caesar but to slaves and employees, perhaps including some of the palace guard who heard of Christ through Paul's imprisonment (1:13).

EXPLORING FURTHER

FELLOWSHIP

The Greek word koinonia which is often translated 'fellowship' occurs in various forms several times in this letter. From the following references and the letter as a whole, what does true Christian fellowship involve?

In these references, the English phrase (from the NIV) translates a form of the word koinonia;

1:5 ('partnership'); 1:7 ('share . . . with me'); 2:1 ('fellowship'); 3:10 ('fellowship of sharing'); 4:14 ('share'); 4:15 ('shared').

Is there a missionary or someone else exercising Christian ministry with whom you or your church could develop the sort of partnership which the Philippian church enjoyed with Paul? In what practical ways could that partnership be expressed and deepened?

JOY

Philippians is sometimes referred to as the 'letter of joy'. In spite of what, and because of what, did Paul rejoice?

COLOSSIANS

'fullness in Christ'

BACKGROUND BRIEFING

Colossae was a modest market town about 100 miles inland from Ephesus and a short distance from the more important city of Laodicea. It was a Gentile area, but unlike Philippi it had a strong Jewish community. The church there was founded not by Paul himself but by Epaphras (1:7), a native of Colossae, who was converted through Paul's ministry in Ephesus. He took the gospel back to his home town and a church was established, meeting in the home of Philemon, a wealthy citizen.

Later, however, the church was troubled by teachers who told them that faith in Christ was not enough. They offered fuller spiritual experiences reached through initiation into secret knowledge and the observance of rituals and severe ascetic practices. This so concerned Epaphras that he journeyed to visit Paul in prison and seek his help (4:12).

This letter was Paul's response. It was carried to Colossae by another native of the town, one of

Philemon's slaves, Onesimus, who had run away and somehow come across Paul, and through whom he had become a Christian.

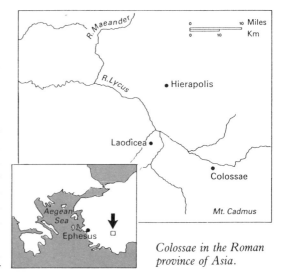

Colossae in the Roman province of Asia.

The Lycus Valley near Colossae. Along this valley Onesimus would have travelled on his way from Rome.

A JOURNEY THROUGH COLOSSIANS

OPENING SECTION

a. Address (1:1–2a)

b. Greeting (1:2b)

c. Thanksgiving (1:3–8)

There is a great deal to thank God for in the life of this young church: faith, love and hope (1:4,5,8). As in Philippians, the heavenward hope is an important element in Paul's thinking. Here faith and love are said to spring from such a hope (1:5). Paul is already eager to stress that the gospel is the truth (1:5,6).

MAIN CONTENT (1:9–4:6)

a. Prayer for growth and fruitfulness (1:9–14)

b. The supremacy of Christ (1:15–23)

He is supreme in his person and status (1:15–19), and therefore effective in the achievement of peace and reconciliation with God (1:20–22). It is possible that *vv*.15–20 are another early hymn.

c. The mystery made known – Christ in us (1:24–2:5)

The heretical teachers spoke of secret mysteries; Paul says that there is indeed a great mystery, but it is a secret which God has now made known – 'Christ in you' (1:27).

To make known this 'mystery' has been Paul's task.

d. Life in Christ (2:6–4:6)

○ In Christ you have all you need (2:6–23).

- continue in him – don't settle for less (2:6–8);
- 'fullness'? – you have it, in Christ (2:9–10);
- 'circumcision'? – Christ has dealt with your sinful nature (2:11–12);
- 'new life'? – God made you alive with Christ (2:13);

- 'regulations'? – you are forgiven through Christ (2:13–14);
- 'spirit forces'? – Christ has defeated them (2:15);
- 'ceremonial laws'? – these are a shadow; Christ is the reality (2:16–17);
- 'worship of angels'? – those who want this are out of touch with Christ, the Head (2:18–19);
- 'rules to control the body'? – these are worldly, and you have died to such things with Christ; anyway, they don't work (2:20–23).

○ Live the life which is yours in Christ (3:1–4:6).

- the heavenward perspective (3:1–4);
- rid yourself of all the practices and attitudes that belong to the old self (3:5–11);
- put on the characteristics of God's people, chosen, holy and loved (3:12–14);
- life in Christ in the church (3:15–17);
- life in Christ in the family (3:18–21);
- life in Christ in the slave-owning household (3:22–4:1);
- share in proclaiming the mystery of Christ (4:2–6).

CLOSING SECTION

a. Personal news (4:7–9)

b. Final greetings and farewell (4:10–18)

Mark has obviously been reconciled to Paul and is now working with him (4:10; cf. Acts 15:36–40).

Even in Rome, Epaphras is working hard for the churches of his home region, in costly prayer (4:12–13).

There was interchange between the church at Colossae and that in the neighbouring city of Laodicea (4:15–16).

Paul's letters were dictated to secretaries, but he often added a farewell in his own hand (4:18).

EXPLORING FURTHER

THE COLOSSIAN HERESY

a. From the arguments against it in this letter, what can be discovered about the content of the teaching which was troubling the Colossian church?

b. Summarise Paul's teaching in this letter about the person and work of Jesus which answers the assertion that he was just one of several spirit beings between mankind and the Almighty God, and that faith in him was not in itself enough to secure salvation.

c. These teachers seem to have made much of knowledge, wisdom, understanding, mystery and fullness. Look at how Paul uses the same words but gives them Christian content.

Many people today hope for such things as 'success', 'security', and 'fulfilment'. How could you take these or other terms which express the aspirations of our society and use them to show the blessings that there are in Christ?

PHILEMON

'better than a slave . . . a brother'

BACKGROUND BRIEFING

To be a runaway slave in the Roman Empire was a risky business – and so was harbouring one. When Paul sent Onesimus back to Philemon he was doing what the law required. On the other hand Paul, a prisoner himself, could hardly compel him to make the journey nor ensure that he would not abscond again. It was as a result of his submitting to the lordship of Christ that Onesimus was willing to return to his earthly master.

The letter which Paul gave Onesimus to carry back with him to Philemon is a model of gentle but strong persuasion. In it we see explored from the inside the tensions which the message of the gospel was creating in the first-century world between the preconceptions, structures and institutions of society and the radical implications of life in Christ.

It was written and despatched at the same time as Colossians.

Turkish villagers near Laodicea. Paul's letter to Philemon establishes the fundamental Christian principle that, whatever someone's position or 'status' in life, each person has infinite value.

A JOURNEY THROUGH PHILEMON

OPENING SECTION

a. Address (1–2)

The letter itself is written in a very personal form, but Paul addresses it not to Philemon alone but also to his wife, the church leader and the church as a whole. Was he intending that, should it be necessary, they would support Paul's appeal and encourage Philemon to respond favourably?

b. Greeting (3)

c. Thanksgiving (4–7)

Sharing your faith is seen by Paul as a means of coming oneself to have a full understanding of every good thing we have in Christ.

MAIN CONTENT (8–21)

The elements in Paul's appeal are:

○ Paul's authority in Christ (8,21);

○ emotional appeal to Paul's own need (9,20);
○ Paul's relationship with and affection for Onesimus (10,11,12,13,16);
○ the change in Onesimus (whose name means 'useful') (11);
○ tactful suggestion concerning Paul's wish for Philemon (13–14);
○ the change in the relationship between Onesimus and Philemon (16);
○ Philemon's relationship with and indebtedness to Paul (17–19);
○ Paul's willingness to pay whatever Onesimus owes (17).

CLOSING SECTION

a. Personal news (22)

Is this another gentle nudge – 'I'll be along myself to see how you have responded!'?

b. Final greetings and farewell (23–25)

EXPLORING FURTHER

PAUL'S ATTITUDE TO SLAVERY

In the Roman Empire in the first century slavery was taken for granted. Slaves accounted for about half the population. Although a century earlier there had been widespread slave revolts centred on vast agricultural institutions worked by large numbers of slaves, in New Testament times most slaves were found in small groups in the better-off households or civic institutions. They were employed in domestic work, various trades, farming, education and medicine. They received accommodation and food, and it was not uncommon for people to choose to enter a household as slaves in order to be provided for. Slaves were not 'persons' before the law, so they had no legal rights, but, in certain regions at least, there were curbs on cruelty, and it was common sense that slaves were more productive if they were treated reasonably well.

This was the setting within which the gospel was preached and its effects began to be experienced.

From the letters which the Christians at Colossae received from Paul, which may well have been read out with both Philemon and Onesimus present as well as all the other slaves and slave-owners, they would have noted:

○ a statement of principle (Colossians 3:11);

Continued on next page

EXPLORING FURTHER continued

○ instructions to Christian slaves (Colossians 3:22–25);

○ instructions to Christian slave-owners (Colossians 4:1);

○ an appeal to a Christian slave-owner on behalf of a Christian slave (Philemon 8–21).

Taking all these together, give an account of Paul's attitude to slavery in the light of the gospel. Other than the 'gospel manifesto' of Colossians 3:11, what principles and considerations affect the practical advice he gives to slaves and owners? You may also wish to refer to Ephesians 6:5–9, another letter which was probably read at Colossae.

EPHESIANS
'all things together under Christ'

BACKGROUND BRIEFING

AN IMPORTANT CITY

The proud city of Ephesus was the gateway to Asia Minor (present day Turkey). In size and importance the city was on a par with Rome or Corinth, and the great temple of Diana which crowned a hill above the city was one of the seven wonders of the world. Paul made Ephesus his base for the evangelisation of the whole region (Acts 18:19–21; 19:1–29:1). He remained there for three years (Acts 20:31) – longer than in any other centre. A strong church was established and leaders appointed.

AN INTRIGUING LETTER

All of this makes the 'letter to the Ephesians' very strange. Not one person in the church is greeted by name, and there is no reference to anything specific in the church's life, even though Paul knew them intimately and must have been deeply interested in all that the church was doing and any challenges it was facing. In some of the ancient copies of the letter, however, the words 'in Ephesus' are missing from the address (1:1).

This, together with the style and the general nature of the contents of the letter, suggests that it was intended not for one church but for several, perhaps as a circular letter to a number of churches in the region. Both Colossae and its near neighbour Laodicea lay within the Asia Minor 'circuit', and it is interesting that the Colossian church was told to read the letter from Laodicea (Colossians 4:16). Could this letter to the church in Laodicea have been their copy of the same circular letter? Both Colossians and 'Ephesians' were to be delivered by Tychicus (Colossians 4:7–9; Ephesians 6:21–22), and there are similarities in content and even in phrases which would be understandable in letters written at around the same time.

A DISTINCTIVE LETTER

In other ways, however, Ephesians is quite distinct among the Pauline letters. Many themes and ideas from the earlier letters, such as the work of Christ, the nature and role of the church, and the relationship between Jews and Gentiles, reappear in Ephesians but are set within a breathtaking vision of the broad sweep of

God's purpose. The language and elegant style seem to some different from other letters.

But none of this requires the conclusion that Ephesians was written either much later or by someone else. Paul's style and vocabulary varied according to the nature of the subject and the intended recipients. He also wrote with the help of different secretaries, perhaps in this instance Luke, who was with Paul in Rome (Colossians 4:14); similarities have been detected between the Greek style of Ephesians and that of Luke's Gospel and Acts.

Free from the necessity to respond to particular crises or address specific situations, Paul set out in this letter to open the eyes of his readers to the scope of God's purposes for the world, the focus of these purposes in Christ, and the role of the Church in God's plan.

A JOURNEY THROUGH EPHESIANS

OPENING SECTION

a. Address (1:1)

The words 'in Ephesus' are missing in some of the oldest manuscripts. It can best be explained as a circular letter, and the name of whichever church was to receive it would be inserted at this point.

b. Greeting (1:2)

c. Thanksgiving (1:3–23)

Much of Ephesians is couched in the language of worship and prayer. This opening section is in two parts. The first (1:3–14) begins like one of the formal Jewish prayers of praise with 'Blessed be God . . .' (1:3). It recounts the blessings they

The vast theatre at Ephesus, with a capacity for 25,000 people. Gaius and Aristarchus, Paul's companions, were dragged into the theatre by an hysterical Ephesian mob (Acts 19:29). The wide colonnaded street, the Arcadian Way, was lined with shops and led from the theatre square to the harbour.

had received from God, blessings uniquely Christian, received 'in Christ' (1:3,4,5,6,7,9,11, 12,13). The second part (1:15–23) sets out the content of Paul's prayer on behalf of those to whom he writes. He longs that they should know God better, understanding more fully the glorious inheritance that God has for them and knowing his incomparable power.

The section closes with a declaration of Christ's lordship over all and headship over the church. It is unusual in Paul's letters to find 'the church' used to refer to the universal body rather than a local congregation, but here Paul is concerned not with particular church situations but with the great sweep of God's purposes for all things. There is a tension between what has already been achieved in Christ (e.g. 1:22) and what has still to be realised (1:10).

MAIN CONTENT (2:1–6:20)

The previous section has already announced both the main theme of God's purpose, 'to bring all things . . . together under one head, even Christ', and Paul's goal for his readers, that they should know God better, especially in terms of his purposes for them and his power at work in them. Now in the main section we see how all this is being accomplished.

a. What God has done in Christ (2:1–3:21)

○ Raised up with Christ (2:1–10).

God's purposes are opposed by hostile spiritual powers (2:1–2). These must therefore be defeated if God's plan is to be fulfilled. Christ has already been declared victor in the spiritual war (1:20–21), and through his victory those who are in Christ receive life and salvation.

○ Made one in Christ (2:11–22).

The wall in the Jerusalem temple which separated the Court of the Gentiles from the inner court, which only Jews could enter, symbolised not only the alienation of the Gentiles from God but also the disunity of humanity. In reconciling the Gentiles to God through the cross, Jesus was also ending the hostility which kept Gentiles and Jews apart, bringing unity in him.

○ The 'mystery' – the Gentiles are included (3:1–13).

God had intended from the beginning that the Gentiles should be included in the promises to his people, but it was only in their day that this had been made clear. It is achieved through the gospel, and the Church is now the means by which God's great plan will be declared to the cosmic powers. The reconciliation to God and to one another which creates the Church is also the manifestation and demonstration of God's purpose for all things.

○ Prayer (3:14–19).

Again Paul prays for his readers, that they might have inner power and fuller knowledge of Christ's love as Christ dwells in them by faith.

○ Ascription of glory (3:20–21).

In an unusual but fitting thought the church as well as Christ is seen as the focus of God's purposes.

b. How we should therefore live (4:1–6:20)

○ Seek unity in the church (4:1–16).

If the church is to be the demonstration of God's great purpose of bringing all things together under Christ, then maintaining unity in the church is a vital and urgent responsibility. Christ-like characteristics should be harnessed to the task of maintaining unity (4:2–3); they are to recognise their unity in the great realities of their life in the body of Christ (4:4–6); the grace which Christ gives to each one and the gifts of the ascended Lord to his church are intended to bring the church to unity as it attains the fullness of Christ (4:7–16).

○ Live according to your knowledge of Christ (4:17–5:20).

In attitude, in word and in deed we must be like Christ.

○ Let Christ's headship control your human relationships (5:21–6:9).

Not only in the household of the church but in our natural households, our acknowledg-

The base of a column from the Temple of Artemis (Diana) at Ephesus. This massive temple was one of the 'seven wonders' of the ancient world.

The consideration of the marriage relationship prompts Paul to comment on the profound union of Christ with his church (5:29–32).

○ Fight the spiritual battle in the power of God (6:10–20).

The account of God's action for us began with his rescue of us from the hostile spiritual powers (7:1–6). Now the section on our responsibilities concludes with the call to stand our ground in this cosmic battle, availing ourselves of all that God has provided for us.

CLOSING SECTION

a. Personal news (6:21–22)

Very little, in keeping with a general, circular letter.

b. Final greetings and farewell (6:23–24)

It is always worth looking for the little touches with which Paul often embellishes the opening , and closing greetings of his letters. Here he adds 'with faith' to the prayer for peace and love (6:23) – a reminder that faith also is a gift from God (2:8).

ment of the lordship of Christ must be expressed in the way we relate to one another (5:21). (The slave-master relationship belonged to the household rather than to what we would understand by the world of work.)

EXPLORING FURTHER

THE CHURCH IN GOD'S STRATEGY

In the letter to the Ephesians, what is God's great goal, and what is the place of the Church within it?

In what practical ways could *a.* your local church and *b.* the worldwide Church fulfil this role more effectively?

UNIT 7

Letters to Leaders

THE PASTORAL EPISTLES

SIMILARITIES AND DIFFERENCES

The three letters 1 and 2 Timothy and Titus are commonly grouped together and referred to as 'the Pastoral Epistles'. They have a number of features in common. All were written not primarily to churches but to colleagues of Paul who were exercising leadership in churches. They contain both advice relating to their responsibilities and personal encouragement; and they are set in the later period of Paul's life.

In other respects, however, they are quite different from one another. In 1 Timothy and Titus Paul is clearly on his travels, looking forward to further ministry, whereas in 2 Timothy he is in prison, expecting imminent death. The letters to Timothy relate to the church situation in Ephesus, which by then was fairly established, but Titus was working in Crete, in a church as yet scarcely formed. It is therefore rather misleading to speak of them as a coherent group separate from the other Pauline letters. Often statements are loosely made about 'the Pastorals' which in fact are accurate for only one or perhaps two of them.

'THE PASTORALS' AND THE ACTS CHRONOLOGY

The personal information about Paul's circumstances which can be gleaned from all three letters is very difficult to fit into what we are told about Paul's movements in Acts. This caused some to suggest that they were actually written much later by someone wanting to adduce Pauline support for a particular position, and produced letters purporting to be from Paul, including a few fictitious personal details to make them look genuine.

Apart from the many other difficulties with that suggestion, it is unnecessary when we accept that Acts does not tell us everything about Paul's activities. We have seen that Paul was probably released from prison after the two years in Rome (with which Acts concludes) and exercised further ministry before enduring a second imprisonment and execution. 1 Timothy and Titus can be fitted into this period of activity, while 2 Timothy would belong to the second imprisonment. Support for this reconstruction is found by contrasting the apparently relaxed regime of Paul's first imprisonment, reflected in the other Prison Letters, and the harsh circumstances in which he wrote 2 Timothy, which make sense in the context of a later, more severe imprisonment.

FAITH AND ORDER ISSUES

It is often stated that the Pastorals reflect a degree of organisation in the church that was not found in the days of Paul's missionary activity. The assumption has been drawn, therefore, that these letters belong to a period when church life had settled down from the exciting 'charismatic' leadership of the apostles to a more routine and structured system. This is misleading on several counts. The references to local church leadership in 1 Timothy and Titus (there are none in 2 Timothy) are concerned not with establishing a structure (in fact the structure which may be discerned is more like that of the Hellenistic synagogues than the developed church order that we have evidence of from the second century) but with the personal qualifications of those appointed to leadership responsibilities.

Timothy and Titus themselves do not fit any 'office' which later emerged in the church, but seem to have been acting as Paul's delegates, performing specific and temporary tasks, including the appointing of local leaders. Further, some degree of structure was essential even from the earliest days of every Christian community, or for that matter of any community.

Another observation is that, instead of teaching the great truths of the Christian faith as many of Paul's letters do, these letters assume that the church's doctrine has already been established and refer to it as fixed and received. In so far as this is the case, it is understandable in terms of the nature of these letters. Paul does not have to teach the faith to his fellow-workers, who have been converted through his ministry and whom he himself has trained. Rather, he writes to encourage them both to hold fast to that which they have learned and to pass it on faithfully to others.

While acknowledging that there are other views, the approach taken here assumes that these letters come from Paul and belong to the later period of his life.

---

1 TIMOTHY

'holding onto faith and a good conscience'

BACKGROUND BRIEFING

Timothy was brought up in Lystra in Asia Minor (Acts 16:1), and was probably converted during Paul's visit there on his first missionary journey (Acts 14). His father was a Greek, but his devout Jewish mother ensured that he was well versed in the Old Testament scriptures. When Paul passed through Lystra again, he asked Timothy to accompany him (Acts 16:2–3), and he became a greatly valued co-worker and friend. He was with the apostle during much of his ministry from then on, and was entrusted with a number of delicate tasks, helping to establish churches founded through Paul's missionary work or going as Paul's representative to tackle particular problems (e.g. 1 Cor 4:17; 16:10–11).

1 Timothy was written while he was in Ephesus, probably about eight years after Paul's stay there. He was not the pastor of the church, nor was he an apostle in his own right. He was there as part of Paul's team, with the task of seeing the church established in its doctrine and practice and with good local leadership.

Personally, Timothy seems to have been rather timid, very conscious of his relative youth, and with a tendency to ill health. He had been warmly commended, however, by his home church, commissioned with the laying on of hands and prophetic confirmation of his ministry, and had inspired not only the apostle's trust but also his deep affection.

1 Timothy contains instructions about the work to be done in Ephesus and also much personal encouragement and exhortation.

Ephesus was an important city and Paul the strategist recognised the urgency of establishing a stable and well grounded Christian congregation there. The remains of the impressive library built a little after Paul's lifetime witnesses to the city's continuing significance in the Roman Empire.

A JOURNEY THROUGH 1 TIMOTHY

OPENING SECTION

a. Address (1:1–2a)

b. Greeting (1:2b)

c. Thanksgiving

There is no formal thanksgiving, but whereas in the letter to the Galatians such an omission was intended to make a point, here it is simply that in this business-like letter to his delegate, Paul gets straight on with the main purpose of his writing.

MAIN CONTENT (1:3–6:19)

This section consists of three passages concerned with teachers of false doctrine, interspersed with various instructions relating to the conduct of life in the Christian community.

The passages which deal with false teachers contain indications of what they were teaching. But there was no need to spell it out to the man on the spot. Paul speaks more of what such teaching produced, and accuses these teachers of unworthy motives. He gives answers to some of the teaching and instructions on dealing with these teachers. On the positive side, however,

Timothy is exhorted not to be side-tracked but to teach the great truths of the faith.

'A good conscience and a sincere faith' (1:5,19) or 'life and doctrine' (4:15) go hand in hand, as is illustrated negatively in the lives of the false teachers and taught positively in the personal exhortations relating to Timothy's own life.

a. The false and the true I (1:3–20)

b. The conduct of church life I (2:1–3:16)

○ The church at worship (2:1–15).

- prayer (2:1–8)
- women (2:9–15)

○ Qualifications for special tasks (3:1–13).

- overseers (3:1–7)
  The Greek term ἐπίσκοπος (episkopos – 'overseer') was used in the Hellenistic world of presiding officials. In the New Testament it is used interchangeably with πρεσβύτερος (presbuteros – 'elder'), the title for the leader in a Jewish synagogue (see 5:17; Acts 20:17,28). The task of the overseers/elders was to 'Be shepherds of the flock of God' (Acts 20:28; 1 Pet 5:1–4). They were the pastor-teachers. Within that role, however, there were different ministries (see 5:17).
- deacons (3:8–13)
  The word διάκονος (diakonos) means 'one who renders service' or 'ministers'. Clearly it is used here of people formally appointed to fulfil particular tasks, though we cannot be certain about what these were.
  In v.11 the Greek word is simply 'the women' and a judgement must therefore be made as to whether Paul meant the wives of male deacons or female deacons.
- Parenthesis (3:14–16)

– in which Paul gives his reason for writing these instructions, and an incidental glimpse of another early Christian hymn (v.16).

c. The false and the true II (4:1–16)

d. The conduct of church life II (5:1–6:2)

○ How to relate to various groups (5:1–2).
○ Widows (5:3–16).
○ Elders (5:17–25).

- salary (5:17–18)
- accusations against elders (5:19–21)
- care needed lest unworthy people be ordained as elders (5:22–25). The passage includes a parenthesis (v.23) on Timothy's health; keeping himself 'pure' does not mean an unhealthy asceticism.

○ Slaves (6:1–2).

e. The false and the true III (6:3–16)

f. The conduct of church life III (6:17–19)

○ The rich (6:17–19).

CLOSING SECTION

Final exhortation and farewell (6:20–21)

The characteristics of the false teaching encountered in Ephesus are again summarised, this time as a personal warning to Timothy not to be like those who have wandered from the faith. Paul's fear both for the Ephesian church and, it seems, for Timothy, is not that they will capitulate to a direct attack but that they might be in danger of drifting away from the true and real to what is empty, futile and therefore ultimately destructive (cf. 1:6; 6:10).

EXPLORING FURTHER

OVERSEERS

Examine the instructions in this letter relating to the overseers/elders. What can be discovered about the qualifications of those chosen; the task involved; how the church was to regard them; their accountability?

From these instructions, what principles do you regard as applicable to people carrying leadership responsibility in the church today?

TITUS

'doing what is good'

BACKGROUND BRIEFING

Titus was a Gentile Christian who was converted through Paul's ministry and worked with him for a number of years. He was given the difficult task of smoothing out the problems that had arisen in the Corinthian church's relationship with Paul, a mission in which apparently he

The island of Crete. About six miles to the right from this view is the harbour of Fair Havens, which Paul's ship reached 'with difficulty' (Acts 27:8).

---

enjoyed considerable success (see 2 Cor 7:5–7, 13–16; 8:16–17). From Paul's letter to him it seems that they had been together in Crete but, when Paul had to move on, he had left Titus behind, charged with setting everything in order and seeing to the appointment of suitable leaders for several new congregations in the island's towns.

Though visitors from Crete were present on the Day of Pentecost, there was no established church there at the time of Paul's visit. The people of Crete were not highly regarded in the ancient world, as their own poet, Epimenides, testified (quoted by Paul in 1:12)! These young churches had to be nurtured in an alien atmosphere.

A JOURNEY THROUGH TITUS

OPENING SECTION

a. Address (1:1–4a)

Paul's concern for the particular problems Titus faced in Crete comes through immediately. The knowledge of the truth necessarily leads to godliness (1:1), and he wants these new churches to be absolutely clear that sound teaching must produce lives which are pleasing to God.

The Cretans were notoriously deceitful; by contrast, God . . . does not lie (1:2).

b. Greetings (1:4b)

c. Thanksgiving

As in 1 Timothy, Paul proceeds directly to the matter in hand.

MAIN CONTENT (1:5–3:11)

Like Timothy at Ephesus, Titus had to appoint elders and deal with false teachers. But more attention must be given amongst these younger congregations to basic ethical instruction, especially to particular groups.

a. Titus's task in Crete (1:5)

b. Qualifications for elders (1:6–9)

c. Troublemakers dealt with (1:10–16)

Already there were some within the church who were leading others astray with ideas derived from Judaism. Titus is to take a no-nonsense approach with them (1:13–14), because of the harm they could do (1:11).

d. What Titus must teach (2:1–15)

That it was necessary to give such instruction indicates the dire moral and ethical milieu in which these churches were being planted.

○ To older men (2:2).
○ To older and younger women (2:3–5).
○ To young men (2.6–8).
○ To slaves (2:9–10).
○ The basis for this teaching (2:11–14).
○ Personal exhortation to Titus (2:15).

e. What Titus must stress (3:1–8)

○ The life of Christians in the world (3:1–2).
○ The essence of salvation (3:3–8).

Paul describes their way of life before receiving salvation (v.3), the means of salvation (vv.4–7a) and that which those who are saved enjoy (v.7b). This must produce a practical result in their lives (v.8).

f. Unprofitable things (3:9–11)

By contrast, Paul indicates the sort of preoccupations which were decidedly unprofitable (v.9) and tells his delegate how to deal with those who cause trouble in such matters (vv.10–11).

CLOSING SECTION

a. Personal news (3:12–14)

Once more, Paul's dominant concern forces its way into an otherwise standard section of the letter (3:14).

b. Final greetings and farewell (3:15)

EXPLORING FURTHER

DOING WHAT IS GOOD

Why, according to this letter, was it so vital that the Christians in Crete should learn to 'do what is good' (2:14; 3:8,14)? Refer both to the theological basis for this way of life and the evangelistic considerations.

---

2 TIMOTHY

'discharge . . . your ministry'

BACKGROUND BRIEFING

When writing this letter, Paul is again a prisoner. His suffering is compounded by loneliness and the pain of the desertion and unfaithfulness of some friends. He is convinced that, though he has been delivered from imprisonments before, this time death awaits him. There is therefore a special poignancy in this letter to Timothy his 'beloved child' (1:2). He wants Timothy and others to hurry to Rome to be with him, but he knows that he might not have the opportunity to speak with him again.

This letter conveys what he is most anxious to pass on to Timothy before he himself departs. As in 1 Timothy and Titus, it is not necessary for Paul to give a detailed account of the content of Christian teaching. Although there are passages rich in doctrine, references to 'what you heard from me', 'the good deposit that was entrusted to you', 'a trustworthy saying', etc, show that Timothy already knew the content of the Christian faith. What he needed was encouragement to hold on to it in the face of opposition and difficulties.

In the Greek world there was a standard form for letters intended to encourage someone to do or not to do something. It included reminders of what had previously been seen or taught

In 2 Timothy 2:3 Paul urges Timothy to 'endure hardship like a good soldier of Jesus Christ.' This carving of a soldier with armour and shield (Eph 6:11) is from Ephesus.

('memory'), instructions about what should be done and what should be avoided ('maxim'), and illustrations of these things in the lives of the writer or others ('model'). All three elements are present in this letter, though it would be a mistake to look for too strict an adherence to a set form in a piece of correspondence which is so personal.

From those whom Paul greets (4:19) we see that Timothy was still in Ephesus when this letter was addressed to him.

A JOURNEY THROUGH 2 TIMOTHY

OPENING SECTION

a. Address (1:1–2a)

While facing death, Paul finds the promise of life that is in Christ Jesus especially significant.

b. Greeting (1:2b)

c. Thanksgiving (1:3–5)

The warmth of affection between these two men radiates from these verses.

MAIN CONTENT (1:6–4:8)

The main section of the letter is given over entirely to encouraging Timothy to fulfil his ministry. Paul is able to present himself as a model for Timothy to imitate. He also draws attention to others, some worthy of imitation and some illustrating what Timothy must avoid. He gives a succession of commands, and urges Timothy to remember both what he has learned and what he has seen of Paul's life and ministry.

a. The context: the gift of God (1:6–7)

Timothy is going to be exhorted to do a great deal, but first Paul reminds him that his ministry and his enabling for it come not from his own resources but from God's grace. It is this charisma ('gift', v.6) which Timothy is to fan into flame.

b. Do not be ashamed (1:8–2:13)

Timothy is urged not to be ashamed either of his witness for the Lord or of Paul, despite his imprisonment, but to be prepared to suffer for the gospel. It is worth it!

○ Exhortation – do not be ashamed (1:8).
○ The gospel of God's grace (1:9–10).

What reason is there to be ashamed of such a wonderful gospel? For Paul and those who feared for his safety it was an immense comfort to recognise that Christ had destroyed death and brought life and immortality to light.

○ Paul's suffering as a herald of this gospel (1:10–12).

If there was no need to be ashamed of the gospel, then neither was there any need to be ashamed of Paul's sufferings, since it was as a herald of the gospel that he was suffering.

○ Exhortation – guard this gospel (1:13–14).
○ People who were ashamed (1:15).
○ One who was not ashamed (1:16–18).
○ Exhortation – be strong in God's grace, and pass on the gospel (2:1–2).
○ Illustrations of endurance (2:3–7).
○ Examples of endurance (2:8–10).

Jesus himself is the supreme example, but in so far as Paul follows Christ and suffers for him, he too is an example worthy of imitation.

○ Incentive to endurance (2:11–13).

c. An unashamed workman (2:14–3:17)

Paul's aim for Timothy is that he should be useful to the Master (2:21). To be so, there is much that he must avoid as well as that to which he must hold.

○ Avoid valueless teaching – correctly handle the truth (2:14–19).
○ Cleanse yourself from ignoble purposes – be useful in noble purposes (2:20–21).

○ Flee evil desires – pursue what is right (2:22).
○ Do not quarrel – gently instruct (2:23–26).
○ A negative model – people who oppose the truth (3:1–9).
○ A positive model – Paul (3:10–13).
○ Summary: equipped for good work through Paul's teaching and the Scriptures (3:14–17).

d. A solemn charge (4:1–8)

○ Accountability (4:1).
○ The task (4:2–5).
○ Paul's example – the work done (4:6–8).

For one who has discharged the duties of his ministry, the appearing of the righteous Judge (4:8, cf. 4:1) is something to be longed for.

CLOSING SECTION

a. Personal news (4:9–18)

Despite his severe suffering and disappointment in those who failed to stand by him, it is the Lord's faithfulness and the heavenward perspective which illuminate Paul's perception of his circumstances, and he concludes with an ascription of glory to God.

b. Final greetings and farewell (4:19–22)

The 'you' in 'Grace be with you' is plural, so Paul is greeting the Ephesian church through Timothy. But the earlier sentence, 'The Lord be with your spirit' is singular, a special prayer specifically for the young Timothy to whom such a weighty charge has been given.

EXPLORING FURTHER

THE EXAMPLE OF PAUL

In what ways could Paul himself serve as a model for his younger co-worker?

DO'S AND DON'TS

Many of the instructions in 2 Timothy have negative and positive aspects. In two columns, list what Timothy is commanded not to do or to avoid alongside what he is commanded to do.

UNIT 8

Letters to Jewish Christians

We meet a varied assortment of documents in the next two units. Though often referred to together as 'The General Epistles', they are in no sense a coherent group. They were written by various authors at different times, with different purposes. Even the designation 'General', indicating a letter addressed not to a particular church or person but to the Church at large, does not hold for all of them. What can be said is that each responds to some threat that a part of the Church was facing and, together, they provide a sobering picture of the challenges from internal problems and external pressures which were part of life for first-century Christians.

In this unit we explore two writings that, in totally different ways, reflect Jewish Christianity. Both are sermons, or, more accurately, 'exhortations'. **James** draws on practical wisdom which would have been very much at home in Judaism and applies it to the Church's life; **Hebrews** is a carefully argued demonstration of the superiority of Christ to all that its readers had previously known in Judaism.

HEBREWS

'fix your thoughts on Jesus'

BACKGROUND BRIEFING

THE AUTHOR

The 'letter to the Hebrews' is surrounded with mystery. There are some personal notes at the end, but it is not in the form of a letter and nowhere are we told either who wrote it or to whom it was addressed. Although it is given the title 'Epistle of St Paul to the Hebrews' in some older Bibles, it was never ascribed to Paul in the first three centuries of the Church's life, and it is most unlikely that Paul was the author.

From the letter itself it is evident that the writer:

○ was thoroughly versed in the Old Testament scriptures (quoting from the *Septuagint*, the Greek version in use amongst the Jews of the Disperson);

○ he wrote excellent Greek;
○ he was known to the recipients of the letter;
○ both he and those to whom he wrote knew Paul's colleague, Timothy (13:23).

Candidates have included Barnabas, Apollos, Silas, and Priscilla and Aquila, but we have to confess that we just do not know.

THE RECIPIENTS

There is equal mystery with regard to the recipients. Again, we may infer some things from the letter:

○ they had been Christians for some time (5:12; 10:32–34; 13:7);

○ they had begun very well but had not fully lived up to that early promise and were now at risk of slipping back and even abandoning their faith;

○ they seem to have constituted a group within a church rather than an entire congregation (5:12);

○ they were familiar with the Old Testament and its priesthood was significant for them.

It has been suggested that they were a group of Jewish Christians in Rome, and indeed Bishop Clement of Rome quoted extensively from Hebrews in a letter he wrote to the Corinthian church in AD 90. But this evidence is not conclusive, as the letter could have been circulated widely before then. Once more, we simply do not know.

THE CONTENTS

For many Christians, however, the greatest mystery is encountered in the letter's contents. We are plunged into a world of elaborate ritual, sacrifice and complex exegesis of obscure Old Testament texts that seems light years away from our contemporary concerns and needs. Many are tempted to pass it over, except for a few stirring or comforting passages, and to take refuge in some other section of the New Testament which seems more accessible and relevant to today. That is a pity, because in fact the message of the letter is vitally relevant to Christians of every generation and background and has a particular urgency today. Furthermore, the message is not hidden! It readily unfolds when we approach the book on its own terms.

The author describes what he has written as a 'word of exhortation' (13:22), i.e. a sermon intended primarily to encourage or stir the listeners to do something. It was customary in synagogue worship for such sermons to follow the Scripture readings (see e.g. Acts 13:15). The best way to approach Hebrews is therefore to begin by asking what the writer wanted to encourage his readers to do. This is not difficult to discover, as he states it very plainly at several points. Then, knowing what the thrust of the sermon is, we will be better able to see the point of the various arguments with which he backs up this plea for action.

> **TO THINK ABOUT . . .**
> Skim through the letter, noting down all that the readers are commanded or encouraged to do, or warned not to do.

THE EXHORTATIONS

The exhortations fit into three main groups, with a fourth at the end of the letter:

○ Beware of disobeying God's voice.
○ Hold on to your confidence in Jesus and his ministry.
○ Persevere in faith to receive what God has promised.
○ Offer worship which is acceptable to God.

Such a message is eternally and universally pertinent. It was directed through this letter, however, to a group of believers for whom the temptation to give up was linked to the apparent security of Judaism. It was a religion protected by law, so if they returned to it they would escape the threat of persecution; as a religious system it seemed to offer an acceptable way to worship and serve God. Had it been wise after all to move outside the covenant people of Israel, to whom the Lord had given the Law of Moses and the ministrations of the Levitical priesthood?

In answer to such doubts, the writer shows that Jesus is the way to God. He is greater than any who have gone before; through him God has spoken more completely and authoritatively; his ministry is superior; and the covenant of which he is mediator is better. The new stands in relation to the old as reality does to shadow.

THE SERMON'S STRUCTURE

The four emphases of the exhortation supply the basic outline for the sermon. In the opening section the first three are introduced, then each in turn is expounded more fully. The fourth is really the goal of the other three but it is made explicit in the closing section. Personal notes and a blessing conclude the letter.

Each emphasis is pressed home in a particular way. The warning to listen when God speaks is based on an exposition of Psalm 95:7–11 which refers to the failure of the people of Israel in the wilderness. The encouragement to hold on to their confidence in Jesus is supported by a detailed comparison of Jesus' ministry with that of the priesthood established to serve in the Tabernacle during the wilderness journey. Great examples of people of faith are drawn from the Old Testament and elsewhere in Jewish history to illustrate the persevering faith that the writer wants to stir up in his readers. The wilderness experience of the people of Israel is again the background as the sermon moves on to speak of acceptable worship. Added to the picture of their meeting with God at Mount Sinai is another Old Testament journey through the wilderness, the 'Way of Holiness' spoken of by the prophet Isaiah which leads the redeemed to Mount Zion.

These emphases and themes are not, however, confined to the sections in which each is most prominent. The various sections are dove-tailed together, so that often a paragraph which concludes the treatment of one idea also introduces the next. Themes are referred to both before and after their main exposition and sometimes two or more ideas are developed together. This makes it more difficult to construct an outline, but like a finely worked tapestry or a skilfully composed piece of music, this 'word of exhortation', for all its great breadth of range and diversity of source and method, is a coherent whole.

The motif of a journey, appropriate for the exhortation to persevere, runs throughout the sermon. There are many similarities with the farewell addresses of Moses to the people of Israel, found in the book of Deuteronomy. On the brink of entering the promised land, Moses reaffirmed God's covenant with the people and encouraged them to press on and inherit what God had promised them, warning them of the consequences of disobedience. This is essentially what the writer of Hebrews wanted to do for his readers, and the wilderness journey thus provided a very natural backcloth.

Your reading of Hebrews will be considerably enriched if you first read some of the Old Testament passages on which the writer draws. For example:

- Deuteronomy 29–31,34 (going on to the promised land);
- Psalm 95 (call to worship and warning against disobedience);
- Psalm 110:1–4 (prophecy of the messianic king-priest);
- Jeremiah 31:31–34 (the new covenant);
- Isaiah 35 (the redeemed return to Jerusalem).

Crowds 'draw near' to the Western Wall in Jerusalem. At the heart of this letter is the good news of a 'better way' by which people may draw near to God.

A JOURNEY THROUGH HEBREWS

JESUS: GOD'S SON; OUR BROTHER; HEAD OVER GOD'S HOUSEHOLD (1:1–3:6)

a. God has spoken to us through his Son – listen (1:1–2:4)

The revelation of God through Jesus is superior to the revelation through the angels, who in Jewish thought were involved in the giving of the Law on Mount Sinai (Deut 33:2). In Israel the authority of Moses was indisputed; he was a prophet 'whom the Lord knew face to face, who did all those miraculous signs and wonders', the like of whom had never since been seen (Deut 34:10–12). But Jesus' authority and the miraculous vindication of his word were even greater (2:1–4).

In his exhortations the writer frequently argues from the lesser to the greater: 'If *this* is the case, how much more will *that* be true.' See 2:1–4 where the punishment for disobeying the message brought by angels is compared with the consequences of disobeying the message declared by the Lord, and also 9:13–14; 10:28–29; 12:7–11; 12:25.

b. We have an effective high priest – trust him (2:5–18)

He who is higher than the angels, God's Son, was made lower than the angels so that he might be our brother.

c. We are God's household – hold on (3:1–6)

GOD HAS SPOKEN – DO NOT HARDEN YOUR HEARTS (3:7–4:13)

Psalm 95 combines an invitation to worship God with a warning against failing to heed his voice. The warning is drawn from the experience of the people of Israel in the wilderness. The writer applies Psalm 95:7–11 to his readers, picking up several of the key words and phrases in the Old Testament text. To fail to listen when God speaks, as he has done in Jesus, is to commit the sin of unbelief, which is disobedience.

a. Beware of an unbelieving heart (3:7–19)

b. Do not fail to enter the promised rest (4:1–11)

c. God's living word judges the heart (4:12–13)

WE HAVE A GREAT HIGH PRIEST – DRAW NEAR WITH CONFIDENCE (4:14–10:39)

a. Our High Priest is able to sympathise and help (4:14–16)

b. Our High Priest is appointed by God (5:1–10)

c. Warning – you are slow to learn (5:11–6:20)

Don't be lazy and fall away; by faith and patience inherit God's promise – He has confirmed it with an oath.

d. Our high Priest supersedes the Levitical priesthood (7:1–28)

In his discussion of the Old Testament priesthood and worship, the writer repeatedly makes the point that what God gave to the Israelites in the wilderness (i.e. the priests of Aaron's lineage and the Tabernacle and its system of worship) was just a copy of the reality which is in heaven (see e.g. 8:5; 9:23–24; 10:1).

Hellenistic thought, derived from Plato, regarded the material world as a reflection of the ultimate reality which was found in the eternal world. The Jewish philosopher Philo of Alexandria had developed this idea in terms of two worlds, of substance (eternal, divine and true) and of shadow (transient, material, imperfect).

For both Plato and Philo the goal was somehow to advance from the latter to the former. In Hebrews, however, the thought is that in Jesus the eternal has broken through into the temporal, the divine into the human, the reality into the world of shadow.

○ Like Melchizedek, he is greater than the Levites (7:1–10).

Melchizedek is mentioned in Genesis 14:18–20 and Psalm 110:1–4. Expounding these scriptures in the manner of a Jewish rabbi, the writer argues that since scripture makes no reference to his birth or death he may be regarded as eternal, a type (i.e. a prefiguration) of Christ.

○ Like Melchizedek, he is a priest for ever (7:11–19).
○ His priesthood is confirmed by God's oath (7:20–22).
○ He is permanently able to save (7:23–28).

e. Our High Priest ministers in heaven and mediates a new covenant (8:1–10:18)

○ A superior ministry in the true sanctuary (8:1–6).
○ A new covenant which supersedes the old (8:7–13).
○ An inner, permanent cleansing (9:1–28).

The priests' ministry of sacrifice under the first covenant provided for a ceremonial, external cleansing (9:1–10); Christ's ministry under the new covenant, by which he offered his own blood, cleanses inwardly and does away with sin (9:11–28).

○ Supersedes the ceremonial law (10:1–18).

PERSEVERE, TO RECEIVE WHAT GOD HAS PROMISED (10:19–12:17)

a. Encouragement (10:19–25)

There is confidence to draw near to God through our High Priest.

b. Warning (10:26–31)

There is a penalty for rejecting the Son of God.

c. Encouragement (10:32–34)

Remember your own early confidence.

d. So persevere (10:35–39)

You will receive what God has promised.

e. Faith in action (11:1–40)

Illustrations from the Old Testament are cited. The point illustrated is not that by believing these people received what God had promised in their own life-times, but that their faith looked beyond this world to the heavenly reality which God had prepared for them (see *vv.*13–16).

f. So persevere (12:1–17)

○ Look at the witnesses and the pioneer (12:1–3).
○ Endure hardship as training which produces good results (12:4–11).
○ Walk the Highway of Holiness (12:12–17) (cf. Isa 35).

WORSHIP GOD IN THE WAY THAT PLEASES HIM (12:18–13:16)

a. Your destination (12:18–29)

This is not Sinai but Zion.

b. Practical worship (13:1–10)

c. Worship as pilgrims (13:11–14)

Such worship is 'outside the camp'. This was the place of disgrace. In a bold juxtaposition of ideas, the writer shows that in Judaism what was intended to be the 'camp', the temporary system of religion for a pilgrim people, had in fact become a 'city'; they thought they had arrived! So when Jesus came summoning them on they rejected him and cast him out of the city/camp.

The true pilgrim people of God must therefore be prepared to leave the apparent security and comfort of their religious system in order to go to the true High Priest and worship through his effective sacrifice. There are echoes of the original call to the Israelites to come out of Egypt and offer sacrifices in the desert (see Ex 3:18;

7:16, etc). For those readers tempted to return to Judaism, the startling inference is that to do so would be akin to abandoning the pilgrimage and following God's leading to receive what he has promised, in favour of the slavery of Egypt.

d. Conclusion (13:15–16)

Worship through Jesus.

CONCLUSION (13:17–25)

a. Personal notes (13:17–19)

b. Blessing (13:20–21)

This wonderful blessing is full of encouragement and draws on many of the sermon's themes. The idea of the Shepherd has not been mentioned previously, but it is very apt. Psalm 95:7 speaks of God's people as his flock, and Moses and Aaron are also referred to as shepherds by whom God led his people through the wilderness (Psa 77:20).

Jesus is, then, the supreme Shepherd, the Lord himself – a further encouragement to listen to his voice and follow him, trusting him to lead to the destination and provide and protect on the journey.

c. Final notes and greetings (13:22–25)

The writer of the letter to the Hebrews calls on his readers to 'run with perseverance the race marked out for us'. Many Roman cities had a stadium where athletic events were held. The ruins of the stadium at Perga is a fine example.

EXPLORING FURTHER

'CONSIDER JESUS'

Summarise what this letter teaches about who Jesus is and what he has done. In what ways is this teaching applied practically to the readers?

How could you use the teaching of Hebrews to show people today the superiority of Jesus over every other ideal or world view?

JAMES

'speak and act as those who are going to be judged . . .'

BACKGROUND BRIEFING

A CHRISTIAN BOOK?

Like many of the New Testament letters, James is written to Christians facing trouble, but in other ways it is very different from most of those we have previously looked at. Instead of following a clear line of thought, it appears at first glance to consist of a collection of sayings and short essays on various subjects, arranged fairly randomly. As such it has been compared to the book of Proverbs and other Jewish 'Wisdom' books, of which many were in circulation in the first century. It has even been suggested that it is more Jewish than Christian.

A closer look, however, reveals a coherent movement in the argument of this practical exhortation. Moreover, when read alongside Jesus' teaching as set out in the Sermon on the Mount (Matt 5–7), we discover that the distinctively Christian elements in this letter are not confined to the two direct references to Jesus (1:1; 2:1) or to 'the Lord's coming' (5:8). Much of James's material seems to be drawn from Jesus' teaching, though often in different words than are found in Matthew (e.g. James 5:12/Matt 5: 33–37).

This would be understandable if the letter were in fact written before the Gospels were widely circulated. Luke tells us that by the time he began to research the Jesus event there were already many written accounts in existence (Luke 1:1–2), and it is possible that the writer of James had access to a collection of Jesus' sayings other than that which Matthew utilised.

Other features of James also point to an early date when the church consisted almost exclusively of Jewish believers. The word used for the Christians' meeting is 'synagogue' (2:2); there is no hint of Gentiles being in the church; and the recipients of the letter are addressed as 'the twelve tribes scattered among the nations' (1:1).

THE AUTHOR

There were two apostles called James, but authorship of this letter has traditionally been ascribed to James the brother of Jesus who, though not a disciple during Jesus' earthly ministry, became a believer and emerged as the leading figure in the Jerusalem church. The letter could have been written to those Christians who were driven out of Jerusalem in the persecution that followed the martyrdom of Stephen (Acts 8:1). The message of the letter would fit such circumstances.

THE THEME

It is not quite accurate to say that James is primarily concerned with behaviour. His theme is **Testing**. The recipients are suffering trials, but he urges them to view these as testing. The outer reveals the inner: what they do and say in these circumstances shows what is in their hearts. It is the Lord himself who will judge, not by external, worldly criteria but by 'the law of freedom' which demands love. So they must not deceive themselves into thinking that their religion will stand the test if in fact their words and actions flow from worldly attitudes and sinful desires.

The theme of Testing gives the letter its structure. It is not split into theological argument followed by practical application, but it is a sustained exhortation supported at every point by strong theological reasoning. There is much which illuminates, for example, the character of God and the nature of true religion.

A JOURNEY THROUGH JAMES

OPENING VERSE (1:1)

Address and Greeting

James assures his readers that they are the true people of God. They are in the diaspora, which could either mean 'scattered among the nations' or 'amongst the [Jews of the] dispersion'.

SEE 'TRIALS' AS 'TESTING' (1:2–12)

a. Trials function as testing (1:2–4)

The Greek words used here for trial πειρασμος (peirasmos) and testing δοκιμιον (dokimion) each have a range of meaning but tend to be used with different connotations. Peirasmos is often negative, something designed to trip you up (another form of the word is translated 'tempt' in 1:13–14), whereas dokimion is positive, proving something genuine (cf. 1 Pet 1 which has peirasmos in *v*.6 for trial and dokimion in *v*.7 for proved genuine). The aim of such testing is to produce good results, so they can rejoice!

b. Qualities the testing requires (1:5–8)

○ Wisdom, faith, sincerity.

c. Values (1:9–11)

○ God's and the world's are not the same.

d. Reward (1:12)

TESTING EXPOSES WHAT IS WITHIN YOU (1:13–27)

a. Evil desire within you produces sin (1:13–15)

b. God's word within you produces good (1:16–18)

c. Human anger within you does not produce a righteous life (1:19–21)

d. God's word planted in you has power to save (1:21)

e. But the word must be put into action (1:22–25)

f. Religion that God accepts (1:26–27)

○ Controlled speech; practical love; freedom from the world's corruption.

LIVE AS THOSE WHO WILL BE JUDGED (2:1–4:12)

a. Illustration – Favouritsm (2:1–11)

○ If you show favouritism you are judging by worldly standards, not by God's (2:1–7).
○ If you show favouritism you yourself are judged by God's standards, and are found to have broken the law of love (2:8–11).

b. Exhortation – live as those who will be judged by God's criteria (2:12–13)

○ Let your words and actions stem from God's values within.

c. Development – how the testing operates (2:14–4:3)

○ Your deeds reveal your faith, or lack of it (2:14–26).

Paul contends that we are saved by faith, not by works (e.g. Rom 3:28; Gal 2:15–16; Eph 2:8), whereas James seems to insist that works are necessary. When each statement is read in its context, however, it is seen that James and Paul do not contradict one another. Paul is talking about the means by which we receive salvation, and draws a contrast between faith-union with Christ and struggling to earn salvation by keeping the moral or ceremonial law. James's theme is testing which separates the genuine from the false, and he contrasts the one who merely says he has faith (2:14) with the person whose faith is evident from his actions. Paul would certainly have agreed that genuine faith has practical results (e.g. Eph 2:9).

○ Your words reveal your character (3:1–12).
○ Your way of life reveals your 'wisdom', whether it is of God or of the devil (3:13–4:3).

d. Challenge to respond to what this testing has revealed (4:4–12)

○ The seriousness of the problem, and the offer of God's grace (4:4–6).
○ Call to repentance (4:7–10).
○ Do not presume to do God's work in judging others (4:11–12).

THE JUDGE IS COMING SOON (4:13–5:12)

a. Do not live presumptuously (4:13–17)

b. Beware, if you are hoarding wealth and exploiting others (5:1–6)

c. Be patient, if you are suffering (5:7–11)

d. Be reverent (5:12)

LIVING IN THE TIME OF TESTING (5:13–20)

a. Pray in all circumstances (5:13–18)

b. Bring back the wanderer (5:19–20)

○ James's last comment perhaps casts light on part of his own motivation in writing to these scattered Christians.

EXPLORING FURTHER

RICH AND POOR

James touches several times on the subject of wealth and poverty. Compare the world's attitude to wealth and poverty with the attitude which James wanted to see in his readers (e.g. 1:9–11; 1:27; 2:1–11; 2:14–17; 4:13–4:4; 4:13–5:6).

What would you say is the prevailing attitude to wealth and poverty in our society? How should Christians be different?

UNIT 9

The Church under Threat

Six letters are included in this unit, **1 and 2 Peter, 1, 2 and 3 John and Jude** – too many to deal with thoroughly. We shall therefore concentrate our attention on 1 Peter and 1 John, both attributed to apostles who had been with Jesus and both applying that witness to situations many years on from the Jesus events. Though we cannot give the same attention to the other letters, brief itineraries are provided for a quick tour!

1 PETER

'God's elect, strangers in the world'

BACKGROUND BRIEFING

Like the letter of James, 1 Peter is addressed to the people of God in the diaspora, but whereas James wrote to Jewish Christians, Peter wrote to a group of churches largely Gentile in composition. One of the features of the letter is the way in which Old Testament designations of the people of God, applied originally to Israel, are used to describe all Christians. The Christians addressed were spread throughout Asia Minor. Paul's mission had extended into this region, and before that people from Asia Minor are mentioned in Acts 2:9–11 as present on the Day of Pentecost. These Christians suffered as a result of their faith. This, it appears, took them by surprise, especially when they could not see that they had done anything wrong to those who were attacking them. The letter sets out to encourage them to stand fast.

Although there was no concerted empire-wide persecution of Christians until the reign of the Emperor Domitian (AD 81–96), there were many instances of more local persecution and hardship long before then, and some vicious

The emperor Nero, during whose reign Christians were severely persecuted.

Reproduced by courtesy of the Trustees of the British Museum

attacks on Christians during Nero's reign (AD 54–68). Since Peter himself was executed by Nero, the letter, if written by Peter the apostle, must date from before AD 68.

THE AUTHOR

Some have argued that Peter could not have been the author because the Greek is too refined for an uneducated Galilean fisherman. Such a view does not allow for the developing of Peter's language skills during three decades of apostolic ministry. Also, the letter was written 'through (or by means of) Silas' (5:12) which could indicate that Silas had a role in how Peter's message was expressed. Peter's authorship is claimed in the letter itself (as well as 1:1 see 5:1, where the writer claims to be 'a witness of Christ's sufferings' and 5:13 which links the author with Mark), and his authorship was acknowledged by early Christian writers.

THE CONTENTS

The reference to baptism (3:21) has encouraged some scholars to regard the greater part of the letter as a baptismal sermon or even a liturgy, with Scripture readings, prayers and instructions to those being baptised. This, however, is rather forced and not necessary. The contents are appropriate not only to those making their Christian profession in baptism but to all Christians, for all are called to live as those who belong to God in a world which does not share that allegiance.

Peter wants to deal with the problem of the suffering that is discouraging his readers, but he approaches it by expounding 'the true grace of God' (i.e. God's dealings with them through Jesus Christ to bring them salvation). As those receiving salvation, they are in relation to God's 'chosen people', but in relation to the world 'aliens and strangers'. In developing the implications of these realities, Peter shows how to understand their suffering and what response they shold make to it.

Christ is presented in this letter not only as the one through whom they are saved but as their supreme example in suffering; he bore up through unjust suffering without retaliating, entrusting himself to God and, having suffered, he entered into glory.

A JOURNEY THROUGH 1 PETER

OPENING SECTION

Address and Greeting (1:1–2)

Christians are both *elect*, the chosen people of God, and *strangers*, people who are in the world but do not really belong. The implications of this are explored in the letter.

The scope of salvation is sketched, involving all three persons of the Trinity.

STATEMENT: SALVATION AND ITS IMPLICATIONS (1:3–5)

a. Praise for the salvation which is to come (1:3–5)

The resurrection of Jesus is the basis for the Christian's hope and faith (cf. 3:21–22).

This letter continually looks forward:

○ to 'the salvation which is . . . to be revealed' (1:5);
○ to 'the day [God] visits us' (2:12);
○ to 'the end of all things' (4:7);
○ to when [Christ's] glory is revealed (4:13; 5:1);
○ to 'when the Chief Shepherd appears' (5:4);
○ to when '[God] may lift you up in due time' (5:6);
○ to when 'the God of all grace . . . will himself restore you and make you strong' (5:10).

b. Joy, even in suffering, because you are receiving salvation (1:6–9)

The trial of suffering is a test which proves faith genuine (cf. James 1:2–3 and note on page 94).

Throughout the letter, *suffering* is closely linked with *glory* (1:6–7; cf. 1:11; 1:19,21; 4:13; 5:1,10).

Although Christ has not yet been revealed (the term expresses better than 'comes again' the conviction that Christ is present now), there is joy now through believing in him.

c. The wonder of this salvation (1:10–12)

Even the prophets through whom Christ was foretold, together with the angels, are straining to know more about this salvation.

Both the Old Testament prophets and the preachers of the gospel were inspired by the Spirit.

d. Live as those who are recieving salvation (1:13–2:12)

In 1:13 there begins a long series of practical commands which continues until 5:9.

○ Be ready to work hard at understanding (1:13).
The orientation of your life should be in setting your hope on this salvation. It will take effort to bring your understanding and attitudes into line with it.
○ Be holy (1:14–16).
The first enemy of the way of life appropriate to those receiving salvation, who are to belong to God, is within you, your own evil desires.
○ Live as strangers in the world (1:17–21).
The second enemy is around you, the attitudes of the world in which you live.
○ Love your fellow Christians (1:22).
○ Instead of false words, crave the living word of God (1:23–2:3).
○ The basis for your lives – you are chosen people, set apart for God (2:4–10).
○ The practical corollary – you are to live as strangers in the world (2:11–12).
The two sources of danger, the sinful desires within and the pagan world around, are again addressed.

DEVELOPMENT: HOW TO LIVE AS 'ALIENS AND STRANGERS IN THE WORLD' (2:13–4:11)

a. Submit to human authorities (2:13–17)

As 'aliens and strangers' Christians are passing through the world rather than permanently residing in it, but they are also in the world for a purpose (2:8). They put self-interest aside in order to commend by their lives the God whom they serve.

The principle of submission is not absolute. It is both enjoined and qualified by such phrases as 'for the Lord's sake' (2:13). Where it would require them to act contrary to God's commands they must, of course, obey God rather than anyone else (cf. Acts 4:19). According to Christian tradition, Peter himself was martyred – not long after writing this letter – for putting his allegiance to the Lord before obedience to the Emperor.

b. Slaves, submit to your masters (2:18–25)

Where this involves suffering unjustly, you have the example of Jesus, through whose undeserved but patiently borne suffering comes salvation. Furthermore, as those privileged to be 'chosen people' (1:1; 2:9, etc) you have to realise that you are 'called' (2:21 – same Greek word as 'chosen') to suffer in that way.

What God commends is not suffering itself, but a Christ-like attitude in those who suffer for doing good (2:20).

c. Wives, submit to your husbands (3:1–6)

Quality of life and character both commends the gospel and demonstrates true spiritual descent from Sarah, the mother of the People of God.

d. Husbands, be considerate of your wives (3:7)

e. All of you, live in harmony with one another (3:8)

f. Repay evil with good (3:9–22)

Again it is Christ who is your example, suffering unjustly for your benefit (3:18). His example is very encouraging because after the suffering came resurrection and exaltation – he submitted to suffering at the hands of human authorities, but now all things are 'in submission to him' (3:22).

The statement that Christ 'went and preached to the spirits in prison' (3:19) has baffled commentators for centuries. Some take it to mean that between his death and resurrection Christ preached the gospel to spirits of human beings who had been disobedient in their earthly lives. They interpret 4:6 in the same way, but it is perhaps more likely that by 'the spirits in prison' Peter is referring to fallen angels, supernatural beings who had tried to corrupt the world and destroy God's work (see Gen 6). Christ's 'preaching' would therefore be the proclamation of his triumph, including victory over supernatural powers opposed to God, in dying to bring people to God (cf. 3:22).

Noah and his family, 'saved through water' in the ark (3:20), serves as an illustration of salvation by the power of God, effected in baptism.

g. Have the attitude of Christ (4:1–6)

h. Live in hope of and in readiness for the end (4:7–11)

○ Keep your head, so that you can pray.
○ Love one another.
○ Use the grace you have received in service for others.

The goal and outcome of such living is 'that in all things God may be praised through Jesus Christ' (4:11). This is a fitting conclusion to Peter's exposition of the life of God's 'chosen people' in a world in which they are 'aliens and strangers'.

CONCLUSION: SHARING IN THE SUFFERINGS OF CHRIST (4:12–19)

Peter now deals explicitly with the issue which has run like a sub-plot throughout the letter, namely 'the painful trial you are suffering' (4:12). Again, he points them to 'the sufferings of Christ' (4:13), but now the Christians' suffering is lifted above the level of imitation of Christ's example to actual participation in those sufferings. This is cause for rejoicing and praise (4:13,14,16). Their response to suffering should therefore be that which they have seen in Christ himself (4:19; cf. 2:23).

FINAL EXHORTATIONS AND ENCOURAGEMENTS (5:1–11)

a. Elders, be shepherds

You will be rewarded (5:1–4).

b. Young men, be submissive

And all of you, be humble – God will lift you up (5:5–6).

c. Cast your anxieties on him

He cares for you (5:7).

d. Be alert and resist the devil

God himself will restore you (5:8–10).

The exhortations flow into a benediction (5:10) and an ascription of praise (5:11) which draw together a number of emphases in the letter:

○ God's grace.
○ The Christians' calling.
○ The eternal dimension, contrasted with temporary sufferings.
○ The link between glory and suffering.
○ Standing firm.
○ God's power.

CLOSING SECTION

Greetings and Farewell (5:12–14)

Peter states his purpose in writing this letter (5:12).

Babylon (5:13) is probably a reference to Rome, especially apt if written during Nero's persecution.

His final greeting, 'Peace to all of you who are in Christ' (5:14b), can be given confidently, even to those who are suffering, in the light of this letter's message.

EXPLORING FURTHER

SUFFERING

The suffering which Peter's readers were enduring caused them to question and tempted them to retaliate in kind.

a. What would they find in this letter to help them understand why they were suffering?

b. What guidance would it have given them on how to respond to that suffering?

Using these points, compose a short letter of encouragement to someone (real or imaginary) who is suffering today for his or her faith.

HOLY AND GODLY LIVES

What can you discover in this letter about the features of holy and godly lives and those things which have no part in such lives?

---

2 PETER

'be on your guard'

BACKGROUND BRIEFING

THE PURPOSE

If 1 Peter was written to encourage Christians facing the external threat of persecution, 2 Peter meets the internal threat posed by false teachers. Within the Christian community (2:1,13,20–21) were those both teaching 'destructive heresies', consisting of invented tales (2:1–3), and living grossly immoral lives (2:13–14,19). This letter warns the church to beware of such people, reminding them of the authoritative sources for the truth they had been taught and exhorting them to holiness of life and growth in grace. One of the important themes of the letter is the coming 'Day of the Lord'. False teachers are to be expected in the last days, and the Christians' hope should be an incentive to be ready.

THE AUTHOR

Although this letter purports to come from 'Simon Peter, a servant and apostle of Jesus Christ' (1:1), the language, tone and content differ so markedly from 1 Peter that many conclude that the two letters could not have been written by the same person. Furthermore it is suggested that certain features of 2 Peter, such as the recognition of Paul's letters as Scripture (3:17), the existence of a body of teaching of which the readers could be reminded (1:12, etc.), and the need to explain the apparent delay in the Lord's coming (3:8–9) are evidence that the letter must date from later than Peter's lifetime. It is also argued that the false teaching which the letter combats was prevalent in the second century.

There are, however, a number of similarities between the two letters, and some difference in language and tone would be expected in letters differing in subject and purpose. We must also bear in mind that 1 Peter was written 'with the help of Silas' (1 Pet 5:12) whereas no such help is mentioned in 2 Peter. As for the 'late' features, such arguments must be treated with some caution because of difficulty in ascertaining precisely when certain ideas were current. We also have to explain the personal allusions in 2 Peter (e.g. 1:12–15; 3:15) and the claim of the author to have been an eye-witness of the transfiguration (1:16–18).

A large number of documents bearing Peter's name were in circulation in the second century, but in the process of establishing which writings were authoritative the great majority of these were rejected, including the so-called 'Gospel of Peter'. 2 Peter, however, was subjected to the same rigorous testing and accepted. At the great Council of Carthage in AD 397 it was ratified along with the other twenty-six writings of our New Testament as part of 'the canonical Scriptures', to be 'read in church under the name of the divine Scriptures'.

A JOURNEY THROUGH 2 PETER

OPENING SECTION

a. Address (1:1)

The reference to a faith as precious as ours suggests that the readers were Gentiles.

b. Greeting (1:2)

MAIN CONTENT (1:3–3:18a)

a. Exhortation (1:3–11)

God has given you all you need, so grow in Christ, and make sure that you are part of God's chosen people.

b. Authentication (1:12–21)

Eye-witness testimony and Holy-Spirit inspired Old Testament prophecy confirm the apostles' message (cf. 3:2).

c. Warning (2:1–22)

God's people of old were troubled by false prophets, and Peter's readers were also plagued with false teachers. Their destructive teaching is made up to entice people into sin, and their lives are catalogues of wickedness, but they will be punished.

d. Explanation (3:1–10)

The 'Day of the Lord' has not yet come, but it will, just as the Flood did. God's concept of time is very different to ours, and he is being patient, wanting everyone to come to repentance so that they will not perish.

e. Exhortation (3:11–13)

In the light of this coming Day of the Lord, live holy lives.

f. Conclusion (3:14–18a)

The three main emphases of the letter are re-iterated:

○ The context: the coming Day of the Lord, and the present opportunity to receive salvation (14–15).

○ The warning: don't be led astray by ungodly people who distort Paul's teaching and that of the other Scriptures (15–17).

○ The positive exhortation: grow in the grace and knowledge of Christ (18a).

ASCRIPTION OF GLORY (3:18b)

---

1 JOHN

'that you may know that you have eternal life'

BACKGROUND BRIEFING

Similarities between this letter and the Gospel of John are apparent from the opening sentence onwards. An extensive list can be drawn up of phrases and ideas which they have in common. If then the Gospel writer was John the apostle, the 'beloved disciple', these similarities of style support the opinion of early Christian writers who unanimously attributed this letter to the same John.

John probably lived in Ephesus for the last thirty years of his life and ministered in various churches in the surrounding region of Asia Minor. Since neither places nor people are mentioned by name in the letter, it may well have been a circular letter to several of these churches.

THE PURPOSE

We have little external evidence of the situation which prompted the writing of this letter. Happily, however, within the letter itself there are declarations of its purpose and indications of John's concerns. John's Gospel was written 'that you may believe that Jesus is the Christ, the Son of God, and that by believing you may have life in his name' (John 20:31). The letter was written to those who already believed, 'so that you may know that you have eternal life' (1 John 5:13).

The reason why such reassurance was necessary is seen in the references in the letter to 'those who are trying to lead you astray' (2:26). These were evidently people who had been within the church (2:19) but had now left and were trying to draw others after them.

We can discover the nature of their teaching from the way John answers it in his letter. They made great claims – to have fellowship with God, to be in him, to be walking in the light, to be sinless – but they continually broke the moral law and disregarded Jesus' commands, claiming that such actions were not in fact sins; they did not show love for the Christians; and they denied that Jesus was truly God and man.

GNOSTICISM

All these features were fundamental to Gnosticism, a system of belief which appeared in several intricately developed forms in the second and third centuries AD and which severely troubled the Church. Taking as its starting point the notion that matter is intrinsically evil and spirit intrinsically good, such an outlook could not accept the apostolic teaching about Jesus, had a very different perception of salvation and also had profound moral implications.

Firstly, God, being spirit and therefore good, could not possibly be joined to a body which is matter and therefore evil. Jesus could not, therefore, be both God and man. Some solved the problem by saying that Jesus only seemed to be human (Docetism), but the teaching which John was challenging held that the divine Christ was not born a man, but took up residence in the body of the human Jesus at his baptism and left him just before he died.

Such ideas are associated with Cerinthus, a teacher who according to tradition was resident in Ephesus at the same time as the apostle John. 'Salvation' became for them an escape not so much from sin as from the body, and they borrowed from Eastern mystery religions the idea of gaining entry into the spiritual realm through initiation into secret knowledge (Greek gnosis). Since it was the body itself which was evil, what it did could be regarded as of little importance, and it seems that John's opponents were refusing to call breaking the law 'sin', claiming that they could somehow attain perfection on the spiritual plane whatever the body was doing.

Against this background, John's purpose was both negative, to expose as false this teaching and those who were perpetrating it, and positive, to encourage the believers in the truth. After a compressed introduction he exposes several false claims and then goes on to expound a believer's true grounds for confidence.

The crucial question is, how may we know that we have eternal life? There are related questions, such as how may we know:

○ that we have come to know Christ;
○ that we are in him;
○ that he lives in us;
○ that we are children of God?

As the letter progresses, it emerges that for John these are all dimensions of the one great reality; to be *born of God* is to have him *living in us* which is *to know him* which is *to be in him* which is *to have eternal life*.

TESTS OF THE TRUE

In order that we may know these things and be able to distinguish the false from the true John

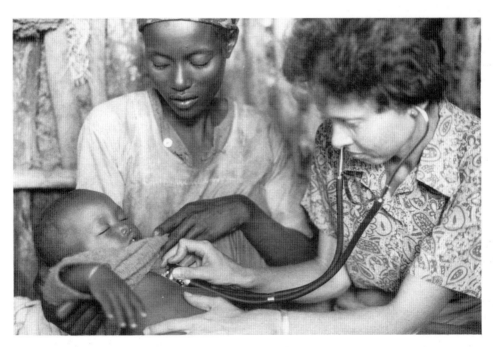

'Dear children, let us not love with words or tongue but with actions and in truth' (1 John 3:18). The picture shows a nurse, funded through Baptist World Aid, serving in Ethiopia.

Photograph by Robert O'Brien and used by courtesy of Baptist World Aid

provides three tests. There is the test of *obedience* to God's commands, the test of *love* for the family of God and the test of *faith*, believing that Jesus is God and man, the Son of God who came in the flesh.

These tests are applied and reapplied in the various sections of the letter, but it transpired that, like the crucial questions, these tests are interconnected; to obey God's commands is to believe in his Son and to love one another (3:23). Thus the argument of the letter builds up, not as a series of steps in a straight line, each following from the previous one and leading to the next, but like strips of papier mache round a sphere, layers of overlapping statements, each of which stands in its own right but which, when taken together, cohere to form a full-orbed representation of true life in Christ.

A JOURNEY THROUGH 1 JOHN

OPENING SECTION

Introduction: the eternal life which we proclaim (1:1–4)

Objections to Jesus' divinity-and-humanity are met head on with these opening statements asserting both Jesus' divine origin and nature and also the reality of his entry into the physical world.

The eternal can therefore be known by human beings – we can have fellowship (shared life) with God.

FALSE CLAIMS EXPOSED (1:5–2:28)

a. Fellowship with God – false claims and the true way (1:5–2:2)

Three false claims (1:6,8,10) are exposed and in contrast the true way to deal with sin (confessing sins and receiving forgiveness made available through Jesus' sacrifice) is explained.

b. The test of obedience (2:3–6)

c. The test of love (2:7–11)

d. John's confidence regarding his readers (2:12–14)

These six statements, grouped almost poetically in two balanced sets of three, express the confidence which is expounded throughout the letter.

The different categories probably refer not so much to different age groups as to stages in Christian maturity.

e. What love for the world reveals (2:15–17)

As in John's Gospel, the conflict between 'the world' and Christ and his people is starkly drawn, but whereas his opponents spoke of a physical world which was evil in opposition to a spiritual realm which was good, that is not the dichotomy which is in John's mind here; he is careful to point out that not all that is spirit is good (see 2:18–27; 4:1–6).

f. The antichrist who lies/the anointing from the Holy One which teaches the truth (2:18–23)

g. Conclusion: remain in him (2:24–27)

To remain in him is to have eternal life. You will remain in him as the message which you heard from the beginning and the anointing remain in you. With these two sources you do not need the other teachers who in fact are trying to lead you astray.

TRUE CONFIDENCE EXPOUNDED (2:28–5:17)

It is by remaining in him that they will be able to have confidence when Christ appears (2:28). John now describes how they may know that they are in him, and thereby have this confidence.

The word 'confidence' (or 'assurance') reappears in 3:21, 4:17 and 5:14, i.e. in the concluding paragraphs of each of the three main sections of this part of the letter. Though each section has a dominant theme, most of the letter's other main ideas can also be found in each one. This is in keeping both with the 'layering' method of presentation, which we have already noted, and with the essential unity of the tests and the reality which they demonstrate.

a. Confidence through obeying his commands (2:29–3:24)

○ Doing what is right shows that you are children of God; going on sinning shows that you are children of the devil (2:29–3:10).
○ Loving your brothers shows that you have passed from death to life; hating your brother shows that you remain in death (3:11–20).
○ Conclusion: you can have confidence because you obey his commands (3:21–24).

This obedience involved believing in the Son of God and loving one another – the three tests are, in essence, one (3:23). Obedience is also the evidence that you are remaining in him (3:24).

b. Recognising the Spirit of God (4:1–6)

In addition to the three tests, a further layer of evidence is provided by the Spirit within us (3:24). This requires a note from John on how the Spirit of God is to be distinguished from other spirits which are in the world.

c. Confidence through living in love (4:7–21)

○ Love, because this is the nature of God (4:7–12).

  Note how the test of love is developed each time it appears: it is evidence of walking in the light (2:7–11); it shows that you have eternal life within you (3:11–15); and now love is shown to be the very nature of God, and therefore to love is evidence that God himself is in you.

○ We rely on God's love, because through the Spirit and the Son we know that we are in him and he lives in us (4:13–16a).
○ Conclusion: we will have confidence because, living in love, we are like him (4:16b–18).
○ Summary: our love derives from God's love and it is also commanded by God (4:19–21).

d. Confidence through believing in the Son of God (5:1–17)

○ Tests of belief, love and obedience interdependent (5:1–5).
○ Witnesses to the Son of God (5:6–12).
○ Conclusion: we have confidence through believing in the Son of God, and in this confidence we can pray and should pray for fellow-Christians who are committing sin (5:13–17).

CONCLUSION: WE ARE IN HIM WHO IS ETERNAL LIFE

a. Three affirmations (5:18–20a)

These sum up what has been argued throughout the letter.

b. Conclusion: we are in the true God, and therefore have eternal life (5:20b)

c. Final exhortation (5:21)

To follow the false teaching leads away from the true God, whom we know in Jesus Christ, to false gods, 'idols'. The exhortation is typically couched in the language of love and fatherly care, 'Dear children . . .'

EXPLORING FURTHER

BELIEVING IN JESUS

What is said in this letter about *a*. **who Jesus is** (his person) and *b*. **what Jesus has done** (his work)? Why is **what we believe** considered by John to be so important?

How would John reply to the view that 'It doesn't matter what you believe, so long as you are sincere'?

---

2 and 3 JOHN

'in truth and love'

'work together for the truth'

BACKGROUND BRIEFING

Unlike 1 John, which is an exhortation in the form of a written sermon, 2 and 3 John are real letters. Each would fit comfortably onto one sheet of papyrus. Both refer to travelling teachers and messengers. Clearly there was a great deal of intercommunication amongst the group of churches in Asia Minor, and John would send out messengers both to greet and to teach the churches. These travelling ministers had to depend on the churches to which they went for food and practical support while they were with them.

These short letters give us a glimpse of two sorts of difficulty which arose in that context. From 3 John we see that John's messengers were not always accepted. There were local church leaders who, perhaps out to consolidate their own power or status, resisted the involvement of 'the elder' in the life of the church and refused to receive either his letter or his delegates. A different problem is evident from 2 John. There were some teachers going round the churches perpetrating a form of the gnostic heresy which 1 John combats, and they were claiming hospitality and support from the Christians.

3 John is a personal letter to a friend named Gaius, commending him for the help he was giving to those whom John had sent, but detailing difficulties that had been encountered with a local church leader, Diotrephes. 2 John is addressed to a church ('the chosen lady and her children'). It warns against giving practical support to false teachers, and thus actually contributing to the harm they do. But the letter is balanced with a positive exhortation to walk in love; the tension between showing love and being concerned for truth has been with the Church since the earliest days.

We do not have enough information to be more precise about the destination of these letters, nor the order in which they were written (though scholars have speculated about it!). The letters do, however, help to fill in the picture of the communities amongst whom John ministered, and in the short compass of 2 John we have a number of beautifully concise statements of the faith and life which he taught which is expounded much more fully in 1 John.

A JOURNEY THROUGH 2 JOHN

OPENING SECTION

a. Address (1–2)

Love for fellow Christians is in the truth, which for John is more than a body of knowledge – Jesus himself is the truth (*see* John 14:6), and he lives in the believers.

b. Greeting (3)

c. Thanksgiving (4)

MAIN CONTENT (5–11)

a. Exhortation – walk in love (5–6)

b. Warning – watch out for deceivers (7–11)

It is the teaching of [about] Christ (9) which is the test: do they acknowledge that Jesus Christ came in the flesh (cf. 1 John 4:2–3)? If not, the believers are not to give assistance to such wicked work (10–11).

CLOSING SECTION

a. Personal note (12)

b. Final greeting (13)

'Your chosen sister' is the writer's own local church, which takes the opportunity to greet the receiving church through him.

EXPLORING FURTHER

TRUTH AND LOVE

These are the great themes of this brief letter. What does it reveal about each of these themes?

A JOURNEY THROUGH 3 JOHN

OPENING SECTION

a. Address (1)

b. Greeting (2)

Of all the greetings found in New Testament letters, this is probably the nearest in form to the typical Greek letters of the time.

c. Thanksgiving (3–4)

MAIN CONTENT (5–12)

a. Gaius praised for his hospitality (5–8)

Hospitality to travelling ministers and missionaries was one of the main ways in which the Christians of the early centuries could exercise partnership in the gospel (8).

b. Diotrephes exposed for his malice (9–10)

c. Demetrius commended to Gaius (11–12)

Here is another typical Johannine summary of the way in which outer behaviour reveals the inner relationship with God (11).

Demetrius may well have been the bearer of the letter.

CLOSING SECTION

a. Personal note (13–14a)

b. Final greeting (14b)

EXPLORING FURTHER

WHAT TO IMITATE

What is there in Gaius's example that is worthy of imitation, and in Diotrephes' that is not?

JUDE

'keep yourselves in God's love'

BACKGROUND BRIEFING

TIRADE AGAINST FALSE TEACHERS

This short letter consists largely of a tirade against false teachers, drawing on examples from the Old Testament and Jewish traditions to describe their sinfulness and the judgement coming upon them. On looking more closely, however, we see that the author is a reluctant combatant. He really wanted to write a positive, encouraging letter about their salvation, but the threat posed by these false teachers compelled him to change his plans (3–4) and write to defend the most holy faith. Even so, the letter opens and closes with warm assurances of his readers' security in God (1–2:21; 24–25). The attitude that he wants them to adopt towards those perturbed by the false teachers, or even already fallen, is one of mercy, seeking to save them (22).

RELATIONSHIP WITH 2 PETER

Much of the central section refuting the false teachers is similar to that found in 2 Peter 2. There could be three reasons for this: 2 Peter has borrowed from Jude; Jude has borrowed from 2 Peter; or both of them have drawn from another document, perhaps a polemic against false teachers which was circulating. In whichever direction it came, it was not slavish quoting. The two passages differ in a number of details. Each includes some things absent from the other, and there are differences in the way the common material is used.

If 2 Peter was written very late then the tendency would be to regard Jude as the source, but if 2 Peter derives from the apostle himself it was most probably written before Jude. In this case Peter would be one of the apostles of our Lord Jesus Christ to whose teaching Jude is able to refer (17–18; cf. 2 Pet 3:3). If his readers were aware of 2 Peter, we could understand Jude's comment that they already know all this (5), and his task was not to introduce new ideas but to reinforce that with which they were familiar, picking out some elements for brief mention and developing others with additional material.

AUTHOR AND RECIPIENTS

So who was this Jude? It was a very common name, but he also describes himself as a brother of James (1). It is reasonable to assume that for the letter to gain credibility and acceptance by the church, it must have come from one of the recognised leaders, and it would be unusual for a writer to introduce himself as someone's brother unless the brother himself were widely known. This writer appears not to have been an apostle himself (17), and for these reasons the most likely candidate from amongst the Judes or Judases encountered in the New Testament is Jude the brother of Jesus (see Matt 13:55; Mark 6:3).

There is nothing to tell us who the original recipients of the letter were, and the sort of problem confronted, of people misapplying the gospel of God's grace in order to give scope to licentiousness, seems to have been sadly widespread amongst the churches from the second half of the first century onwards.

A JOURNEY THROUGH JUDE

OPENING SECTION

a. Address (1)

In the face of these threats, the description of the readers as called . . . loved . . . kept . . . would have been very comforting. The kept and keep motif recurs in various ways throughout the letter (*see* 6,13,21,24).

b. Greeting (2)

MAIN CONTENT (3–23)

a. Jude's reason for writing (3–4)

b. Polemic against the false teachers (5–19)

The reference to the dispute between the archangel Michael and the devil (9) and the quote from Enoch (14–15) come from extra-biblical Jewish writings. Paul was also willing to find support from sources outside the Scriptures for points he wished to make (e.g. 1 Cor 15:33; Titus 1:12).

c. Positive exhortation (20–23)

CLOSING VERSES
Ascription of glory (24–25)

EXPLORING FURTHER

IN THE BATTLE

The threat described in Jude's letter is very real, but his readers are not helpless. What can they do, and on what can they depend (3; 20–23; 24–25)?

UNIT 10

The View from the Throne Room

UNDERSTANDING THE BOOK OF REVELATION

Some Christians turn to the book of Revelation with avid interest, searching eagerly amongst its mysterious visions for clues to the unfolding of present and future events. To many others it appears odd, even disturbing, with its menagerie of strange creatures and its images of war, plague and destruction. It seems best to them to set it aside and get on with their Christian lives with the help of less obscure parts of the Bible!

The first group are in danger of going to the book with their own agenda, looking in it for what they want to know rather than allowing it to say what the author wanted his readers to know. The second group must not ignore an integral part of the witness of Scripture and miss out on its vital message for want of the effort

required to listen to it. It is certainly worth hearing.

The approach that we have taken with all the writings we have explored so far is to come to each on its own terms, trying to discover first what sort of literature it is, whether letter, sermon, treatise or a combination of such elements, and then reading it as such. In this way the structure and methods appropriate to each form act as vehicles for the content, and we are better able to see exactly what it was that the writer wanted to communicate, and how it would have come across to the first readers. Taking the same approach with Revelation will allow the book to disclose its meaning in the way the author intended and will save us from a great deal of misunderstanding.

WHAT IS IT?

APOCALYPSE

The opening verses of the book tell us precisely what it is. It is announced as a Revelation (1:1). The Greek word αποκαλυψις (apokalupsis) has the general meaning of 'disclosure'. That is comforting; the purpose of the book is to make something known, not to make it obscure! Apokalupsis was, however, also used in a technical sense to denote a particular type of literature, and it is in this sense that John's readers would certainly have understood it.

Scores of 'apocalypses' were produced between the middle of the second century BC and the end of the first century AD. They were Jewish writings claiming to reveal what God had done in history and what he would do as he brought about his ultimate victory and eternal kingdom.

In times of trouble and distress for the Jewish nation, these writings affirmed that God would act, his people would be vindicated and those who were oppressing them would be defeated and punished.

Although to outward appearance this was not the way that history was moving, in fact God's secret plan had been in operation from the beginning and was steadily progressing to its great culmination. This hidden plan had been made known to select individuals, and was now revealed to God's people to encourage them because the goal was very near. They were to hold on steadfastly, looking for the coming Kingdom of God which would be perfect and blessed. This kingdom was sometimes portrayed as the rule of God achieved on the earth, usually centred on Jerusalem; more often, however, it was only in a new heaven and new earth that the Kingdom of God would be fully realised.

The Apocalypses purported to have been given in dreams or visions to great figures of the past, such as Enoch, Abraham or Moses, and their accounts of history are therefore presented as predictions of the future. Their language is highly symbolic, drawing not only on pictorial images from Jewish traditions but also on the mythologies of Babylon and Persia where the Jews had been in exile. Numbers have special significance and history is schematised as a succession of distinct periods of time, which are different phases of God's plan.

John's readers knew, therefore, what to expect when presented with a book described as an Apocalypse. It was going to draw back the curtain on God's purposes and reveal what was really going on beneath the surface of historical events; they were going to read of God's Kingdom, what it was like and how it would be realised. In addition they knew that the language of the book, along with special numbers and schemes, had to be taken *not literally* but *symbolically*.

PROPHECY

Those first readers found, however, that this writing differed in two very important respects from the many other Apocalypses in circulation. First, it is described as prophecy (1:2; cf. 22:6, 7,9,10,18,19). First-century Jews believed that, with the last of the Old Testament prophets, prophecy had ceased. It would be one of the signs of the Last Days, the epoch of God's decisive intervention in history of which the Old Testament prophets spoke, that the Spirit of Prophecy, the living voice of God speaking directly to his people, would again be heard. John's claim that what he writes is prophecy therefore indicates not just that it is a direct message from God but that he and his readers were already in the Last Days.

From this follows the other major difference from other Apocalypses; John writes in his own name (1:1,4,9ff), and describes the way he received his vision and was told to communicate it in terms similar to the calling of Old Testament prophets. This was not, then, a scheme of history from the perspective of some great figure of the past to whom was revealed the distant future; it is what God made known to the first readers' own contemporary, God speaking there and then directly to their own generation about 'what must soon take place' (1:2,3).

TESTIMONY

John is at pains to stress that he simply 'testifies to everything he saw' (1:2). The book is 'the testimony of Jesus Christ' (1:2). Like the phrase 'revelation of Jesus Christ' (1:1), this has two meanings: Jesus Christ is both the source and the subject of the revelation and testimony. The same is true of the book as prophecy, for the testimony of Jesus is the spirit of prophecy (19:10). As the curtain is drawn back on God's purposes it is Jesus who is revealed. John's task – and that of his readers – is to bear faithful witness to him.

LETTER

Having introduced the book as apocalypse, prophecy and testimony, John proceeds to set it in the form of a letter. There is the address (1:4a), greeting (1:4b–5a), rather than a thanksgiving, an ascription of praise (1:5b–6), followed by the main content, and then a final greeting (22:21).

This is an important reminder to us that, like the other New Testament letters, this document was addressed to real people at a particular time, and it had real meaning for them in their situation. As with the messages given through the Old Testament prophets, we can expect the visions given to John to reach beyond the immediate situation of his contemporaries. But our interpretation of the book of Revelation must be disciplined by taking seriously the context in which it was written and what it communicated to those to whom it was first addressed.

WHEN WAS IT WRITTEN, AND BY WHOM?

DATE

The circumstances described in the letters to the churches (chapters 2–3), together with the fact that John was on Patmos, a small rocky island off the coast of Asia Minor where prisoners were detained, point to a time when the Church was suffering persecution from the authorities. Apart from sporadic local hostility, there were three periods of state persecution of Christians, during the reigns of the emperors Nero (AD 54–68), Vespasian (AD 69–79) and Domitian (AD 81–96). Most scholars find the last of these to be the most likely. Under Domitian the cult of emperor-worship was promoted vigorously and Christians who refused to participate were regarded as a threat to the state, and extensively persecuted. The date of around AD 95 accords with the view of early Christian writers.

AUTHOR

The writer identifies himself as John (1:1,4,9; 22:8). John the Gospel writer, the 'beloved disciple' of Jesus, probably lived to a great age and exercised much of his ministry in Asia Minor with Ephesus as his base. Revelation has commonly been attributed to him, but there are difficulties with this. For one thing, the writer of Revelation never describes himself as an apostle. However, the writer of the Gospel and Letters of John does not use 'apostle' as a title for himself, and in Revelation the writer is eager to stress to his readers that this wonderful vision has been given to one of themselves, their 'brother and companion in suffering . . .' (1:9).

More seriously, whereas the Greek language and style of the other writings which bear the name

The remains of a temple at Pergamum dedicated to the emperor Trajan, reminding us of the cult of emperor worship which prevailed when Revelation was written.

of John are possibly the most beautiful in the New Testament, that of Revelation is rough and grammatically incorrect. We have already noted, in considering the documents attributed to Paul and Peter, the role played by the skilled secretary who may not only have written down what the author dictated but also polished the style. John might have had such assistance in Ephesus, but not on Patmos.

When we look at the ideas expressed in these writings there is of course much material in the Apocalypse that is not found in the Gospel and Letters, but there are also marked similarities. Consider, for example, the references to Jesus as 'the Word of God' (19:13; cf. John 1:1) and 'the Lamb' (5:6,8,12 etc. cf. John 1:29), the importance given to the blood and sacrifice of Jesus (5:9–10, etc. cf. 1 John 1:7; 2:2; 4:10), and to testimony (1:2,5,9; 2:13; 6:9, etc. cf. John 1:15; 21:24; 1 John 1:2). In itself, this cannot prove that one author was responsible for them all, but it does demonstrate a close connection in thought between the Gospel and Letters of John and the Revelation.

TO WHOM WAS IT WRITTEN, AND WHY?

THE RECIPIENTS

As a letter, the Revelation is addressed to **the seven churches in the province of Asia** (1:4). These were real churches, and the content of each individual message is often related to actual features of the town and church addressed, such as the regional centre of emperor-worship situated in Pergamum (2:13 – 'where Satan has his throne') or the banking centre, clothing industry, and reputation for eye ointment in Laodicea (3:18).

THE PURPOSE

There was a definite message for each of these seven Christian communities relevant to the condition and circumstances of each. Faced with external attack and internal error they were encouraged to recognise that **Jesus was amongst them**, the eternal sovereign Lord, King and Judge, and that he saw what they did and what was happening to them. They were urged to **remain true and faithful**, even if this cost them their lives, and to **maintain purity of life and**

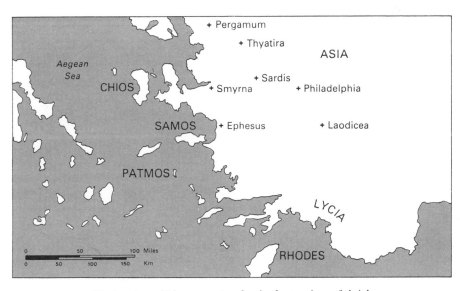

The location of 'the seven churches in the province of Asia'.

The Roman theatre at Pergamum is the steepest ever constructed.

doctrine. They were **promised the blessings** which Jesus had won for them by his victory, if they themselves overcame with him.

The number seven also carries great significance as a symbol of completeness. Just as 'the seven spirits' (1:4) is a way of denoting the Holy Spirit in his completeness and perfection, 'the seven churches' are, in a sense, the whole Church.

There was a particular message for each individual church, but each as a part of the whole Church was to receive the whole message (1:4,11). Revelation was from the first intended not only to speak directly to these named congregations but to present **a message** which would transcend those individual circumstances and speak **to the whole Church of Jesus Christ**.

HOW SHOULD WE INTERPRET IT?

With a work of such complexity it is hardly surprising that no two interpreters of Revelation agree in every detail. It is possible, however, to group the various interpretations according to their views of the book's relation to real historical events.

REVELATION AND HISTORY

Some see the whole book as referring to John's own day. The visions were descriptions of the circumstances which the Christians were enduring at the end of the first century, expressed in coded language to escape detection by the imperial authorities; this is the **Preterist** interpretation. Others regard all or most of the book as a description of the period of time immediately preceding Christ's return (**Futurist**). **Historicist** interpreters find in the book an account of world history from John's time right through to Christ's return. In contrast some take the 'poetic' or **Idealist** approach, which does not look for any relationship between the visions and real historical events and people, reading them rather as artistic presentations of great themes, such as the ultimate triumph of good over evil.

LITERARY STRUCTURE

Interpreters also differ markedly on their understanding of the book's literary structure, i.e. how the message is developed. Some regard the successive **visions as a chronological sequence**, beginning with John's day in chapters 2–3 and moving through time to the new heavens and new earth in chapters 21–22. An alternative is to regard some of the **visions as parallel accounts**, portraying different aspects of the same events or phases. The seven seals, the seven trumpets and the seven bowls would then describe the same series of seven events. An extreme version of the parallel approach is to **divide the whole book into groups of seven units**, each series of seven beginning in John's immediate circumstances and progressing to the culmination of God's purposes in the final unit of the series.

LETTING THE BOOK SPEAK

The approach we have adopted here, of letting the book itself tell us what it is, does not answer all the questions of interpretation, but it provides valuable pointers to the intended meaning of the book.

As **Apocalypse**, its purpose is not so much to recount what will take place on the surface of human affairs but to draw back the curtain which veils God's purposes from view, and to show what is *really* going on, and what the end of it all will be. In other words, the various pictures are not saying 'This is what is or will be taking place', but 'This is what is or will be taking place *means* from the perspective of God's rule and purpose'.

As **Prophecy**, it is the voice of God speaking directly to John's contemporaries. But, just as his readers understood that the messages given through the Old Testament prophets reached beyond their immediate generation and, especially, found full realisation in Christ, so they would not necessarily expect to find everything portrayed in the book in their own immediate circumstances. What John is commanded to write encompasses both what is now and what will take place later (1:19).

Yet as a **Letter** it spoke to real people in particular circumstances, and the recipients were certainly intended to recognise references to their own experiences and those who were persecuting them.

An example of a stone aqueduct which brought water into the city of Laodicea which, unlike nearby Colossae and Hieropolis, had no natural water supply. The water was warm at its source but became lukewarm, and in the process of cooling calcium carbonate was deposited on the walls of the pipes as can be seen in the picture.

MESSAGE FOR THE FIRST READERS

What would those who first read this book have taken its message to be? The following is a summary.

WHO IS IN CONTROL?

The book of Revelation declares that **Jesus is Lord**. The glorious figure who speaks with John has characteristics not only of the Son of Man but of the Ancient of Days, the Lord God himself. He has won the victory by his death and now the unfolding of the world's destiny is in his control. He is worshipped by angelic beings and by the people of God, and his Kingdom is eternal.

WHY IS THERE SO MUCH TROUBLE AND DISTRESS?

Revelation shows that **the world is being punished for its rebellion against God**. Conquest, war, famine, and death are an expression of God's righteous anger against sin and a summons to the people of the earth to repent.

WHAT WILL HAPPEN TO THE CHURCH DURING THIS TIME OF DISTRESS?

There is the assurance that **God's people will be protected**. They will not escape the suffering that has come upon the world, but the complete number of God's servants will be marked as belonging to him, and what they endure cannot take their salvation away from them; in fact it prepares them for heaven.

WHY IS THE CHURCH ESPECIALLY UNDER ATTACK?

As the curtain is drawn back, it becomes clear that **there is a war going on**. War has taken place in heaven between Christ and Satan. Satan has been defeated, but now he tries to continue the war on earth, empowering his agents to attack Christ's followers.

Ruins of the synagogue at Sardis.

HOW SHOULD CHRISTIANS RESPOND?

The answer is, with **patient endurance and faithfulness**. In particular, Christ's people are to **bear witness** to their Lord. It is by their testimony, even though it lead to physical death, that they share Christ's victory and overcome Satan.

A baptistry excavated in Pergamum and dating from the late first century.

Photograph by John Nicholson

WHAT IS IT ALL LEADING TO?

The punishment meted out on the world will culminate in the **destruction of the world system that is opposed to God. Jesus will come as conqueror** to defeat Satan's forces, and even on this earth there will be **vindication of those who have given their lives for Christ**. Yet this is not the final state. **Satan will be destroyed, the present universe will disappear**, and then will come the **judgement of all humankind**. Then the full blessedness and perfection of the life of God with his people will be realised in **a new heaven and a new earth**, the city of 'the Lord God Almighty and the Lamb'.

A coin from Thyatira. The divine blacksmith, Hephaestus, dressed as a workman and seated at an anvil, gives the finishing blow with his hammer to a helmet for Pallas Athene, the goddess of war, who stands ready to receive it. On the other side of the coin is the head of the emperor. The command to 'render to Caesar the things that are Caesar's and to God the things that are God's,' received a new significance when Caesar claimed divine attributes and demanded worship.

A JOURNEY THROUGH REVELATION

OPENING VERSES

a. Prologue (1:1–3)

The book is announced as Apocalypse, testimony and prophecy. It is for Christ's servants, given by God through Jesus, an angel and John, and its purpose is to show them 'what must soon take place'.

'The revelation of Jesus Christ' (1:1) – can mean either revelation which is given by Jesus or revelation about Jesus. Probably both meanings are intended.

'Blessed is . . .' (1:3) – the first of seven beatitudes woven into the book (cf. 14:13; 16:15; 19:9; 20:6; 22:7,14).

b. Address (1:4a)

c. Greeting (1:4b–5a)

'The seven spirits' (1:4) – a good example of the symbolic use of the number seven to denote completeness and perfection; the phrase refers to the one Holy Spirit.

'Jesus Christ' (1:5) – is introduced in terms which are directly relevant to the church under persecution at the hands of the state: as the 'faithful witness' he is their example; he was put to death, as some of them might be, but he rose again; all earthly rulers come under his supreme sovereignty.

d. Doxology (1:5b–6)

In place of the Thanksgiving which would follow in a standard letter, there is an outpouring of praise to Jesus. It is again what he achieved by his death which is stressed.

MAIN CONTENT (1:7–22:17)

WORDS OF ENCOURAGEMENT (1:7–8)

A brief prophecy about Jesus' coming is followed by a statement from God himself. For God to make himself known as the Alpha and the Omega, the first and last letters of the Greek alphabet, indicates both his eternal being and his absolute sovereignty over beginning, end, and all that is between.

JOHN'S CALL TO PROPHESY (1:9–11)

John briefly mentions the experience that he shares with his Christian contemporaries – **suffering**, which for him included exile to Patmos, the **kingdom of Christ** in which they shared, despite their rejection by the kingdoms of the world, and **patient endurance**. All these are to be important themes in the book.

His reaction to the vision and the Lord's reassurance (1:17) are similar to experiences of Ezekiel (Ezek 1:28) and Daniel (Dan 8:17–18; 10:7–19).

VISION OF CHRIST AMONG THE CHURCHES (1:12–3:22)

The description of Christ is drawn largely from Old Testament sources; see especially Daniel 7:9,13; 10:5–6. Features of God's anointed agent of salvation are combined with those of the Lord God Almighty himself to reveal Christ's nature.

It is also significant that in this first vision Christ comes to where John is. The struggling Christians to whom John wrote were being assured that the Lord Jesus, though exalted and glorious, was right there amongst them, and that he had messages for them.

John is to write what he has seen, 'what is now and what is to take place later' (1:19). There is both the present and the future in the visions of this book.

The letters to the seven churches are remarkable in how specific they are concerning the circumstances of each church, but there is also a comprehensive message to the whole Church. Each letter consists of:

○ **A self-description of Christ**, drawn from the earlier vision of Christ and pertinent to the message which follows.
○ **The condition of the church** as seen by Christ, and the action that he calls for.
○ **The call to** him who has an ear to **hear what the Spirit says** to the churches, widening the scope of the message's application from the particular church to the whole Church.
○ **Promises to him who overcomes** which at the end of the book are seen to be fulfilled in the blessings of Christ's final victory and the new Jerusalem (19–22).

VISION OF THE THRONE IN HEAVEN (4:1–5:14)

a. Worship of the Creator (4:1–11)

John is now invited to 'come up here' and he finds himself in the very throne-room of Heaven (cf. Ezek 1; Isa 6:1–3; 1 Kings 22:19). Here God reigns in glory, majesty and power, and is worshipped continually as the eternal God, the Creator of all things.

○ 'twenty-four elders' (4) – probably representatives of all God's people;
○ 'four living creatures' (6) – heavenly beings.

b. The scroll (5:1–5)

God holds a sealed book filled to capacity with his purposes for the world (cf. Ezek 2:9–10). It is announced that someone has won the right to open the book and thereby both reveal and set in motion what was written in it – 'the Lion of the tribe of Judah, the root of David' (5:5), titles of the Messiah (Gen 49:8–10; Isa 11:1,10).

c. The Lamb (5:6–14)

When John looks for the conquering Lion, he sees 'a Lamb, looking as if it had been slain' (5:6). It is by his sacrificial death that Jesus has won the victory. He is worshipped by those who surround the throne as the Redeemer who has accomplished God's gracious purposes for humankind (5:9–10); innumerable angels join the chorus of praise (5:11–12), and finally the whole of creation sings out in adoration of 'him who sits on the throne and . . . the Lamb' (5:13).

○ 'seven horns and seven eyes' (5:6) – perfect in power and wisdom. Remember that these pictures are intended to reveal the nature and significance of who they depict, not the physical appearance!
○ 'the prayers of the saints' (5:8) – are carried right to the throne of Heaven and have their place in its worship.

VISIONS OF JUDGEMENT AND SALVATION (6:1–7:17)

This is the first of three series of seven judgements (cf. Lev 26:18,21,24,28).

a. The first six seals (6:1–17)

The opening of the first four seals unleashes four horsemen (cf. Zech 1:8) who bring conquest, war, famine and death on the earth (6:2–8).

On the opening of the fifth seal the souls of Christian martyrs are heard crying out to God, asking how much longer it will be until they are vindicated. The answer given is that their number is not yet complete; there will be more martyrs before the final victory. This is one of a number of 'not yets' in the book, conditions which still have to be fulfilled before the final realisation of God's Kingdom.

Martyrdom, faithful witness leading to physical death, is an important theme in Revelation. Even in this brief episode we note:

○ 'under the altar' (9) – such death is, from heaven's perspective, an offering to God;
○ 'slain because of the word of God and the testimony . . .' (9) – such faithfulness will meet with violent hostility from those who oppose God;
○ 'given a white robe' (11) – speaks of proven worthiness and purity (cf. 7:14).

The opening of the sixth seal is followed by cataclysmic events which suggest that the very cosmos has begun to disintegrate and cause the people of the earth from the highest to the lowest to flee to the mountains in terror of the Day of God's wrath (6:12–17). In such terms Old Testament prophets described the 'Day of the Lord', in which God would finally act against the unrepentant wickedness of humankind (e.g. Isa 2:19; 34:4; Joel 2:10–11; 2:30–31. Cf. also Matt 24:29).

b. The sealing of God's servants; the multitude in white robes (7:1–17)

The question 'who can stand?' (6:17) leads to an interruption in the succession of Seal visions by two other visions concerned with the Church in this time of distress. The first (7:1–8) indicates that before these terrible events are permitted to take place, all of God's people will receive his mark; this will be their protection (cf. Ezek 9:4).

○ '144,000' (4) is a symbolic number used here to represent the total number of God's people; 12 (a complete number) × 1000 (= a great many) × 12 tribes = the complete number of the whole people of God.

The second vision (7:9–17) is from the vantage point of the future and shows God's people who have come through this period of acute distress. Drawn from every people group on the face of the earth, they now rejoice in victory ('palm branches') and praise God for his salvation. They now live continually before God and enjoy true wholeness in purposeful service and God's complete protection and provision.

○ 'washed their robes . . . in the blood of the Lamb' (7:14) – their fitness to join the company of heaven is achieved through Christ's sacrifice.

c. The seventh seal (8:1–5)

Up to this point heaven as portrayed in the visions has been filled with the tumult of worship. Now there is 'silence' (8:1), either the awe of heaven at what is revealed on the breaking of the seventh seal or possibly to enable the prayers of God's people on earth to be heard. These prayers (4) play a part in bringing God's majesty, power and judgement onto the earth (5) in what is the culmination of all these judgements.

○ 'thunder . . . rumblings . . . lightning' (5) – manifestations of God's majesty and power. (Cf. Ex 19:16; Rev 4:5)
○ 'earthquake' (5) – usually denotes judgement.

This vision links the seal series with the trumpet series which is to follow (8:2,6).

VISIONS OF JUDGEMENT AND WITNESS (8:6–11:19)

The sounding of the trumpets heralds a second series of judgements. The pattern is similar to that of the seven seals, but there is an intensification in their severity.

a. The first six trumpets (8:6–9:21)

The first four (8:7–12) are even more terrifying than the first four seal judgements, since they involve not merely what human beings can do to one another, but cataclysmic events. These are reminiscent of the plagues on Egypt (Ex 7–11).

On the sounding of the fifth and sixth trumpets God ceases to hold back demonic hosts which are waiting to afflict humankind (9:1–19), although he sets limits to their activity (9:5,10, 15). They are not allowed to destroy utterly, for the goal of these preliminary judgements is to warn and call to repentance. Yet such is the persistence of rebellion that even after all this the people of the earth still choose demons and idols before the Lord (9:20–21).

○ 'a star' (9:1) – in this instance the star represents an angel;
○ 'the Abyss' (9:2) – a dwelling place of demons;
○ 'locusts' (9:2) – cf. Ex 10; Joel 1:2–2:11. It is not vegetation which these locusts harm, but people who do not belong to God. The appearance of these creatures is suggestive of the barbarian warriors who threatened and ultimately overran the Roman Empire.
○ 'seal of God' (9:4) – God's mark of ownership (7:3). Cf. Ex 8:22–23, etc.;
○ 'Abaddon . . . Apollyon' (9:11) – both names mean Destroyer;
○ 'the four angels' (9:14) – these are evil angels who have been bound.

b. The angel and the little scroll; the two witnesses (10:1–11:14)

As in the seals sequence, there is an interlude after the sixth item which deals with the Church. The first vision (10:1–11) assures the Church that she will not have to endure indefinitely. Once the seventh trumpet has sounded, God's purposes will be fulfilled (10:6–7). But meantime the Church has a vital role in a world whose opposition to God is reaching its climax.

Just as the prophet Ezekiel was given a message for the rebellious people of his generation, sweet for one who longed for God's Kingdom but bitter in its warning of judgement (Ezek 2:1–3:15), so John is given a message for his time (10:7–11). The Church shares this task of witness, for which Christ's people will be kept safe and given power (11:1–6). When their task is done they will be killed and scorned, but they will experience resurrection. The effect of their testimony, along with the accompanying judgements, will be the conversion of many (11:7–13).

○ 'little scroll' (10:2) – not the book of the world's destiny (5:1), but a message which John is to proclaim (cf. Ezek 2:7–8; this is also the witnessing task of the Church described in 11:1–14);
○ 'seven thunders' (10:3–4) – thunder speaks of judgement. John is, however, forbidden to write down what was thus expressed, a reminder that there is more to God's purposes than even the visions of Revelation make known;
○ 'swore by him who lives for ever' (10:6) – a most solemn oath confirming beyond doubt that there will be no more delay (10:6);
○ 'Take it and eat it . . .' (10:9–10) – completely master its contents (cf. Ezek 2:8–3:3);
○ 'measure . . . count' (11:1) – indicates that they will be kept safe;

○ '42 months' (11:2) – a stylised period of three and a half years which is the same as 1260 days (11:3). This seems to have become a conventional designation for a period of terrible wickedness;

○ 'the beast . . . from the Abyss' (11:7) – Satan's agent on earth; see 13:11–18; 17:3–18;

○ 'three and a half days' (11:9) – a very short period compared with the length of their time of witness (three and a half years).

c. The seventh trumpet (11:15–19)

In confirmation of the angel's promise (10:6–7) the sounding of the seventh trumpet is greeted by the declaration that Christ's Kingdom has begun (11:15,17). Now is the time for things long predicted but which belong to the final consummation of the Kingdom; God's wrath on the nations; judging the dead; rewarding the faithful; destroying the destroyers of the earth (11:18).

Like the seventh seal (8:3–5), the seventh trumpet brings a manifestation of God's majesty and power (11:19), but this time it derives not from the incense altar (prayer) but from within the temple where the ark of the covenant is seen (symbolising God's faithfulness in keeping his covenant with his people). The judgement is also intensified.

VISIONS OF WAR (12:1–14:5)

a. The woman, the dragon and the male child (12:1–17)

We are now in the middle of the book, and also at what many see as its theological centre. We are shown Satan attempting to destroy Christ but being himself defeated, and going off to vent his rage for a limited time in an ultimately futile campaign against Christ's people. The message is clear; Christ's victory has already been won, though in the present age Satan is still lashing out at those who belong to Christ. They also win the victory through Christ's sacrificial, redemptive death, and by their faithful witness to him (12:10–12).

○ 'a woman' (12:1) – the faithful people of God who awaited the Messiah;

○ 'dragon' (12:3) – Satan (12:9). Egyptian, Babylonian, Persian and Greek religion all contained stories conforming at least in part with the pattern of an evil dragon trying to destroy at birth a child who was destined to slay him, and of the child's escape and victory. John uses the pattern to illuminate Satan's vicious opposition to Christ and his decisive failure.

○ 'a son' (12:5) – Jesus;

○ 'taken care of for 1260 days' (12:6; also 12:14) – cf. 11:1–3, the period of wickedness during which, however, the Church is kept safe to fulfil its witness;

○ 'Michael' (12:7) – a mighty Archangel; cf. Dan 10:12; 12:1;

○ 'they overcame' (12:11) – both past and future! Christ's victory has already been won, and so the victory of Christ's people, which is the same victory, has also been won, even though John's readers must endure in order to enter into the experience of that victory;

○ 'the rest of her offspring' (12:17) – the faithful people of God.

b. The beast which comes out of the sea (13:1–10)

The two beasts encountered in chapter 13 depict the allies upon whom Satan calls in his resolve to destroy the Church of Christ. The 'beast coming out of the sea' is a world power which John's readers would have recognised as the Roman Empire, and especially the emperor himself. They would have identified the 'beast coming out of the earth' who causes people to worship the first beast as the official religious institution of the Roman state.

The dragon with the two beasts make a demonic trinity mirroring in evil the triune God and demanding from the world the worship and allegiance which belong to God alone. The first beast is therefore an 'Antichrist', counterfeiting certain features of the true Christ and claiming his place.

John's readers would have had no difficulty in seeing the emperor, demanding worship and waging war against the Christian Church, in that role, but the nature of the Satanic opposition to Christ depicted here is not restricted to that one particular historical expression.

○ 'a beast . . . seven heads and ten horns' (13:1) – this beast shares the nature of Satan (12:3). The seven heads are explained in 17:8–11 as rulers;

○ 'leopard . . .' (13:2) – cf. Dan 7:2–7;

○ 'seemed to have had a fatal wound' (13:3) – counterfeiting the resurrection of Jesus. There was a strongly held belief at the end of the first century that the emperor Nero, who had died in AD 68, would return to life. The suggestion in 17:11 may well be that in the emperor Domitian the characteristics of Nero were found again so that he is not only an eighth king, but also one of the seven.

○ 'and to conquer them' (17:7) – Christians must expect the apparent defeat of imprisonment and death (see also 13:10) at the hands of the beast;

○ 'patient endurance and faithfulness' (13:10) – what their response should be.

c. The beast which comes out of the earth (13:11–18)

○ 'like a lamb . . . like a dragon' (13:11) – seeks to deceive by appearing like a lamb (cf. Matt 7:15). This second beast is referred to elsewhere as 'the false prophet' (16:13; 19:20; 20:10);

○ '666' (13:18) – a trinity of imperfection (6 falls short of 7);

VISIONS OF VINDICATION AND JUDGEMENT (14:1–20)

a. The 144,000 on Mount Zion (14:1–5)

In contrast to the fiendish scenes which precede it we now see the true Lamb with those who are marked as his own. The worst devices of the dragon and the beasts have not succeeded in wresting from the Lamb one of those sealed with his name and the name of his Father.

○ 'a new song' (14:3) – to praise God for a new experience of deliverance;

○ 'did not defile themselves with women' (14:4) – did not commit spiritual adultery by worshipping the beast (cf. 14:8).

b. Three angelic pronouncements (14:6–12)

Three dimensions of God's judgement are revealed by these statements:

○ it will affect the entire world, and the announcement of coming judgement is a call to all people to turn to God (14:6–7);

○ the world system or institutions opposed to God will be judged (14:8);

○ individuals will be judged (14:9–11).

c. Comments from heaven (14:13)

Christians facing the prospect of martyrdom are assured that to die in union with Christ is to be blessed. Nor is what they have done forgotten in heaven. This glad confidence is in contrast to what awaits the worshippers of the beast (14:9–11).

d. The harvest of the earth (14:14–16)

This first of two harvest pictures symbolises the judgement of the world as a general ingathering of all, righteous and wicked alike (cf. Matt 13:30). Christ himself effects this judgement at the time appointed for it.

e. The winepress of God's wrath (14:17–20)

The second picture is of the gathering of the enemies of God for punishment (cf. Isa 63:2–6).

○ '1,600 stadia' (20) – approximately the length of Palestine.

FINAL VISIONS OF JUDGEMENT (15:1–19:10)

The description of the final series of seven judgements contains many allusions to the plagues with which Egypt was afflicted before the Exodus, both in the nature of the punishments and in the failure of the people to repent (16:1–21). Fittingly, this series is introduced with a section which looks beyond the judgements to the victory of Christ's people, and shows them singing a song of deliverance beside the sea, as the people of Israel did beside the Red Sea (Ex 14:29–15:21).

a. The song beside the sea (15:1–4)

○ 'the song of Moses . . . and the song of the Lamb' (15:3) – the deliverance of the people of Israel from Egypt provides an analogy for the deliverance of God's people from a sinful and rebellious world. 'The Lamb' is the great leader and deliverer, and his people have come through the terrible time of conflict on the earth (15:2; cf. 13:14–17).

b. Preparation for the seven last plagues (15:1,5–8)

Seven angels are handed cups, the content of which is 'the wrath of God' (15:7). The pouring of these upon the earth will bring to completion the punishment on rebellion and sin which warns of the Final Judgement which lies ahead and calls the people of the earth to repentance.

c. The seven last plagues (16:1–21)

Just as the trumpet judgements intensified the seal judgements, so these bowl plagues carry further what was heralded by the trumpets. How this development should be understood is, as we have seen, one of the points on which interpreters differ. Some see a chronological sequence while others assert that these are three descriptions of one set of events.

The most important point is, however, not in the chronology but in the nature of what is portrayed. War, destruction, 'natural disasters', cataclysmic events and demonic activity are all indicators of a world in rebellion against God, its Creator and Ruler. They should awaken the nations and people of the earth to the seriousness of their condition and stir them to repent, but, as in ancient Egypt, there is stubborn refusal to acknowledge God (16:9,11).

○ 'Armageddon' (16:16) – the hill of Megiddo, a strategic location overlooking the plain of Jezreel, the site of many ancient and modern battles, including the defeat of the Canaanite kings by the Israelites under the prophetess Deborah, celebrated in another song of deliverance (Jud 5:19);
○ 'severe earthquake' (16:18–21) – compare the intensity of this seventh judgement with the seventh seal and the seventh trumpet (8:5; 11:19). This time the manifestation comes in response to the voice of God on the throne (16:17);
○ 'the great city' (16:19) – probably representative of world civilisation as a political, economic and commercial system organised without God and resisting his rule. When this city is destroyed, all the cities of the earth fall with it.

d. The great prostitute who sits on the beast (17:1–18)

We are given first a vision (17:1–6a) and then an explanation (17:6b–18). The 'beast' is again the agent of Satan, identified as human rulers. Their rebellion against God's rule will culminate in joining together under the authority of the beast to wage war against the Lamb and his people (17:13–14), and they will be defeated. The 'prostitute' is a city full of luxury and wealth but doing evil and corrupting the rulers of the earth. She has been responsible for the death of many of Christ's witnesses. The explanation includes the rulers of the earth turning on this city to destroy it (17:16). Thus the beast itself becomes an instrument of God's judgement (17:17).

e. The fall of Babylon declared and greeted on earth (18:1–24)

The ruin of this great city which has been the pride and security of the world is greeted by praise in heaven and laments on earth. An angel announces Babylon's fall (18:1–3) and another, declaring that this is apt recompense for her sins, warns God's people to separate themselves from Babylon and not share her punishment (cf. Jer 51:45). There is mourning for Babylon from kings (18:9–10), merchants (18:11–17a) and seafarers (18:17b–20) (cf. Ezek 27:35–36). Finally an angel summarises the judgement and the reasons for it: this city has led the entire world astray, and has murdered God's people (18:21–24).

f. The fall of Babylon greeted in heaven (19:1–10)

In contrast to the mourning on earth, heaven resounds to shouts of praise: the ruin of Babylon has revealed God's salvation, glory, power and justice (19:1–5).

Now a further implication of the fall of Babylon is made known; that which resists God's rule has been destroyed, and his Kingdom has now come. The time of the preparation of Christ's people to be with him is now completed, and 'the wedding of the Lamb' is ready to take place (19:6–9).

John's instinctive reaction to such wondrous news is to fall down to worship the one through whom it is given, but he is forbidden to do so. The angel, like John and his fellow Christians, is a witness. It is God alone who is to be worshipped and it is God's Spirit who inspires all witness to Jesus (19:10).

○ 'the wedding of the Lamb' (19:7) – God entering into a marriage relationship with his people is pictured by the Old Testament prophets (e.g. Isa 54:5–10; Hos 2:16,19–20). Those who belong to Christ are both the bride (19:7) and the guests (19:9).

VISIONS OF CHRIST'S VICTORY AND THE HOLY CITY (19:11–22:6)

The book moves to its conclusion with portrayals of Christ's final victory and the blessedness which this victory inaugurates.

a. The rider on the white horse and his victory over Satan's agents (19:11–21)

Jesus comes in glory and might and meets the combined forces of the rulers of the earth who have gathered under the sway of the beast and the false prophet (see 17:12–14). Christ is completely victorious, and the two agents of Satan are confined to eternal punishment.

○ 'the great supper of God' (19:17) – in contrast to the wedding supper of the Lamb (19:9) is this gruesome picture of judgement, with vultures summoned to the carnage (19:21);
○ 'the fiery lake of burning sulphur' (19:20; cf. 20:10,14–15; 21:8) – this picture of a place of rejection and punishment draws on standard images found in apocalyptic writings which are at least in part derived from the appearance of the valley of Gehenna outside Jerusalem. It had horrible connotations from its use for human sacrifice and in new Testament

times it was the city's refuse tip, where fires smouldered continuously (cf. Matt 5:22).

b. The thousand years (20:1–6)

On the defeat of his forces, Satan himself is not immediately destroyed, but is consigned to the Abyss for a period of time. During this time those who had been killed because of their witness to Christ are resurrected and exercise a priestly reign with Christ. This vision expresses the conviction that even though earthly authorities have not accepted the witness of Christ's people, their testimony will yet be vindicated on earth. It is the status of the martyrs which is emphasised, rather than the character of their reign or of life on earth during it.

○ 'a thousand years' (20:2,3,4,5,6,7) – another symbolic number, indicating a long time; the martyrs' period of vindication will far exceed the period of humiliation (11:7–11);
○ 'the first resurrection' (20:5–6) – a selective resurrection specifically to raise up the martyrs;
○ 'the second death' (20:6) – the death which follows the Last Judgement for those who do not belong to God (20:15).

c. The final overthrow of Satan (20:7–10)

Even after the reign of Christ and his people the nations of the earth have a bias towards rebellion and when Satan is released from his thousand year imprisonment he is able to lead them in opposition to the people of God. Satan's army is utterly destroyed, and the devil is himself cast into the place of punishment and rejection which already holds his two agents.

○ 'Gog and Magog' (20:7) – here symbolise the nations of the world gathered against God's armies (see Ezek 38–30).

d. The judging of the dead (20:11–15)

Earth and sky have now come to the end of their usefulness, and they disappear. All that remains is a throne, and all who have ever lived must gather before it to give account. The issue of life or death is seen to hang upon the contents of books. One set of books records everything which each person has done, and according to its contents, each is judged; the other book is 'the book of life', listing all who belong to Christ: those whose names are found there enter into life.

Thus the twin principles of accountability for one's life and dependence for salvation on what Christ has done are both affirmed. Once this is done death itself and the place of the dead are cast away.

○ 'the book of life' (20:12,15) – cf. Exodus 32:32–33; Psalm 69:28; Daniel 12:1–2 for the Old Testament idea of a book listing those who have a place in God's Kingdom. It is referred to as 'the Lamb's book of life' in 21:27, indicating that it is through the Lamb's redeeming work that people come to be there.

e. The Holy City, the bride of the Lamb (21:1–22:6)

Sky, earth and sea have now passed away, and it is in the setting of a new heaven and earth that the final purpose of God to dwell with his people in blessedness and perfection is realised. God himself declares his new work of creation (21:5). It is the end which he, 'the Alpha and the Omega', has planned from the beginning. To the one who thirsts for him it is his free gift; for the one who overcomes it is the promised inheritance; but there is no place here for the wicked (21:6–7).

The bride is quite deliberately contrasted with the great prostitute (17:1–19:3). For example, one has the character of Satan, the other is the creation of God; the prostitute is bedecked in worldly luxury and wealth, the bride radiant with the brilliance of God's glory; one corrupts the nations of the world and brings them down with her to destruction, the other is the source of healing and life for the nations. Babylon is destined to fall, the New Jerusalem will remain for ever.

The description of the city (21:9–22:5) conveys the ideas of beauty and permanence, perfection and worth. It is a manifestation of the nature of God. God himself, the Lord God Almighty and the Lamb, is its temple, its light and the source

of life. God's people are there to serve him, to see him and to be his. The promises made to churches in the throes of the conflict to encourage them to hold on and overcome are all gloriously fulfilled here. They – and we – can depend upon it; God himself is the source of the information. And it will be soon (22:6).

○ 'I am making everything new' (21:5) – cf. Isaiah 65:17–19;
○ 'he carried me away to a mountain . . . and showed me the Holy City' (21:10ff) – cf. the experience of Ezekiel who was taken to a mountain and shown features of the ideal Jerusalem and its temple (Ezek 40–48);
○ 'temple' (21:22) – the temple was given by God as a means whereby mankind could meet with him. There is no need for this in the Holy City, for the Lamb has demolished all barriers between mankind and God and there God's people live face to face with him.
○ 'the glory and honour of the nations' (21:27) – affirms that even though it was usurped and pillaged by the beast and the prostitute there is glory and honour in the nations which will find its true place and value when offered to God in submission.

FINAL WORDS OF VERIFICATION, ENCOURAGEMENT AND WARNING (22:7–20)

The vast, awe-inspiring vision is complete. The disjointed nature of the succession of little paragraphs with which his letter tumbles to a close gives the impression that John is still reeling from it all. He wants, however, to impress upon his readers the importance of paying attention to what they have read, to reiterate warning and invitation and above all to leave them with the words of Jesus himself, 'Behold, I am coming soon!' (22:7,12,20). 'Amen!' says John, 'Come, Lord Jesus.'

BENEDICTION (22:21)

'As in Revelation, so in history; grace shall have the last word' (G.R. Beasley-Murray).

EXPLORING FURTHER

THE REVELATION OF JESUS CHRIST

Trace the fact that it is essentially Jesus Christ who is revealed in this book.

THE LETTERS TO THE SEVEN CHURCHES (2:1–3:22)

Summarise what these letters reveal about

a. the nature of the one who speaks to the churches;

b. what pleases and dipleases him about the churches;

c. what is promised to those who overcome.

WORSHIP

Examine the songs of worship recorded in Revelation, to discover *a*. who is worshipped, and *b*. for what.

Compare the focus and motivation of this worship with that of the next service at which you are present.

FAITHFUL TO THE POINT OF DEATH

Go through Revelation from the standpoint of a first-century Christian struggling with the demand from the state authorities that all should worship the emperor or face punishment and even death. From what perspective does the book help you to see your own situation as a late first-century Christian? What is there in the book which encourages and perhaps warns you?

What help can this book offer to a Christian entering the twenty-first century?

FOR FURTHER STUDY

This study guide has provided a brief introduction to most of the New Testament documents. Working through it you will have acquired a general awareness of their contents, some knowledge of the first-century world in which those documents came into being and some skill in reading and understanding them. The manual has been self-contained; other than the Bible itself, it has not been necessary to refer to any other book. You will, however, find a great deal of help in various books which will aid you as you go on reading and seeking to understand the New Testament.

Amongst books on the **method of reading and understanding the Bible**, G.D. Fee & D. Stuart *How to read the Bible for all its worth* (SU/1983) is exceptionally helpful. The authors demonstrate the different approaches demanded by the various types of literature contained within the Bible and give guidelines both for discovering what the writers intended it to mean and for applying it to our own circumstances.

Reference books such as **Bible handbooks** and **Bible dictionaries** can throw light on words, situations and concepts that you come across in reading the New Testament, and many give helpful introductions to each of the biblical books. The many available include *The Lion Handbook to the Bible, The Hodder Bible Handbook* and *The Illustrated Bible Dictionary* (IVP) (three volumes).

A good **concordance** is another helpful reference work which enables you to track down words and passages. They range from handy sized volumes to vast exhaustive tomes, some of which give the Hebrew and Greek terms which the English words render. In Bible Study, as in most other DIY activities, the better the tool the more satisfactory will be the result! The standard works are still older concordances such as *Young's Analytical Concordance* (Lutterworth), which has the Hebrew and Greek, and *Cruden's Complete Concordance* (Lutterworth). But they were of course compiled for the AV, which is a problem if you are not familiar with that translation. The NIV is now served, however, by an *NIV Exhaustive Concordance* and *NIV Handy Concordance* (Hodder & Stoughton).

New Testament Introductions discuss the origins, background and main ideas of New Testament writings. The treatment of such matters as who wrote the documents, to whom they were written and why, and what sort of literature they are may seem rather technical, but the intention is to enable us to understand the New Testament documents on their own terms, and the effort expended in using these Introductions is richly repaid in a fully understanding of the Bible. John Drane *Introducing the New Testament* (Lion/1986) takes a documentary approach and is full of helpful illustrations; D. Guthrie *New Testament Introduction* (IVP/1970) gives a very thorough treatment of each book; L.T. Johnson *The Writings of the New Testament* (SCM/1986) has drawn on many of the most helpful insights of recent scholarship to produce a fascinating introduction to the New Testament documents.

Commentaries on individual books usually begin with a section dealing with questions of introduction and then go through the book in detail. There are 'devotional' commentaries which set out to apply the message of the book, and 'exegetical' commentaries which concern themselves with the language, text and ideas of the book in its historical, linguistic and theological context. Some combine the two approaches. William Barclay *Daily Study Bible* (St Andrew Press) and *The Bible Speaks Today* (IVP) are series which aim both to draw out the contemporary relevance of the New Testament, and to ground their exposition in careful exegetical work. These contain many insights, and Barclay's knowledge of historical settings and the connotations of particular words can bring the text alive for the reader. It would be well worth, however, acquiring one thorough exegetical commentary for each book. These may not seem so readable as the BST series or Barclay, but as you study the New Testament you want a commentary which will help in the primary task of unearthing the original meaning of these writings. If that work is done accurately, the application of the message to our own lives follows naturally.

In deciding which of the many available commentaries is most useful to you, look at how the author deals with one of the really difficult passages in the book in question. Are the possible meanings discussed fairly, so that you understand all the options, not just the one which the author favours? Are you given information about the Greek terms, the historical setting, the theological significance? Are you informed if some important ancient manuscripts give an alternative reading of the text, and are you alerted to how such a variant would affect the meaning? Look also at the introductory section and ask yourself if it helps you to understand the occasion and purpose of the book. And of course, if it is to be useful to you, it has to put all this across in a way that is intelligible to you!

The *Tyndale New Testament Commentaries* (IVP) try to deal with the technical matters fairly briefly and accessibly, and concentrate on opening up the meaning of the text with some pointers to its application. Other series of exegetical commentaries, some of which are more demanding of the reader than others, include the *New International Greek Testament Commentary* (Eerdmans), *Anchor Bible* (Doubleday), *New Century Bible* (Oliphants), *Black's New Testament Commentaries* (Black/ Harper), *New London Commentaries* (Marshall, Morgan & Scott; and the *International Critical Commentary* (Clark).

There are also other **CTP Manuals** which will take you further in your understanding of the New Testament, including the Gospels. Titles recommended are:

John Barfield, *Enjoying the Greek New Testament*;

John Drane, *The Gospels*;

Donald Monkcom, *John's Portrait of Jesus*;

John Morgan-Wynne, *John's Gospel* – a special study;
> *The Mission and Message of Jesus*;
> *The Epistle to the Romans*.